AF814211

# IZZ AL-DIN AL-SULAMI

## *His life and Works*

**Sayyid Rizwan Ali**

KITAB BHAVAN
NEW DELHI-110002

**KITAB BHAVAN**
Publishers, Distributors, Exporters & Importers
1784, Kalan Mahal, Darya Ganj
New Delhi-110002 [India]

Phones : (91-11) 3274686, 3277392, 3277393
3258006, 3258007, 3258008
E-Mail : nasri@nda.vsnl.net.in
Website : http://www.kitabbhavan.com
Fax : (91-11) 3263383

First Published in India . . . . . .1898

ISBN 81-7151-255-0

Book Code No. I00320

*Printed & Published in India by :*
Nusrat Ali Nasri for Kitab Bhavan
1784, Kalan Mahal, Darya Ganj
New Delhi-110002 [India]

# *Table of Contents*

## CHAPTER—IV

## AL-SULAMI AND MYSTICISM



## CHAPTER—V

## RELIGIO-POLITICAL ACTIVITIES



## CHAPTER—VI

## CHARECTER AND PERSONALITY

ACKNOWLEDGEMENTS

I am deeply indebted to my supervisor, Professor A.J. Arberry, who took great interest in my subject and spared no encouragement and help to make my research possible.

My thanks are due to Mr. J. Mattock for his reading through the text and for his valuable remarks and suggestions. To Mr. J. Leveen I am thankful for translating several descriptive passages from Latin, German, and French catalogues of Arabic MSS.

# PREFACE

I have chosen for my study a person who in spite of his rare personal and academic qualities has greatly been neglected by authors.

'Izz al-Dīn al-Sulamī, my author, was among those very few who greatly influenced their age. It would not be an exaggeration to say that he was the man of the seventh century A.H. (13th A.D.) as a religious reformer. His acute sense of righteousness and extra ordinary moral courage in criticising and rebuffing the absolute Sulṭāns and powerful viziers of his time amazed and deeply impressed the early authors.

In modern times, two Arab essayists have introduced this particular aspect of 'Izz al-Dīn's life to the general reader in their two essays. Nevertheless, his high academic qualities remained unknown or known only to a very limited circle of specialised scholars.

By choosing this author for my study I have trodden virgin soil. Excluding my own previous work in Arabic, this study is the first of its kind in either a European or an Oriental language.

I had planned to discuss my sources separately and in detail, but this plan I dropped later because of the growing bulkness of the dissertation. However, a few words seem necessary in this respect.

Those who are familiar with the nature of the biographical dictionaries in Arabic know how little information is supplied, generally in them; and how this insufficient information is arranged in bits and pieces, so that to get a vivid and complete portrait of a person is almost impossible. The later biographers tediously repeat their predecessors, very seldom adding any new information.

However, I have endeavoured to produce a complete and live image of the author, putting my information in chronological order. My frequent recourse to the historical sources — that is, the annals of the period — was of great help in this achievement.

I have viewed my sources in historical order and have referred, preferably, to the earliest and most original of them. References to later authorities have only been made to complete some gap or confirm controversial or important points.

Fortunately, one of my author's sons wrote a monograph on his father's life. It is by no means a full biography, nor was it meant to be so. However, it has preserved a good deal of information on his relationship with the monarchs of his time. Another original and perhaps detailed biography was written by Qāḍī 'Abd al-'Azīz al-Hakkārī (d. 727 A.H.). This is unfortunately not extant.

Al-Subkī (d. 771 A.H.) has always been considered the earliest and most comprehensive source for my author. He is still the most comprehensive source, since he incorporated the above-mentioned monograph by 'Izz al-Dīn's son in his *Ṭabaqāt*. By his own account, al-Subkī is no longer the earliest authority. For I have discovered another earlier and original source. He is Qutb al-Dīn al-Yūnīnī (d. 726 A.H.), in his supplement to *Mir'āt al-Zamān* of Sibṭ Ibn al-Jauzī. This author provides us with some first-hand accounts of 'Izz al-Dīn's life which are not found in any other biographical work.

I have also kept a critical eye on my sources. Their statements have been accepted only after careful scrutiny and comparison with the more scrupulous and reliable authors.

I had agreed with my supervisor to translate my previous Arabic work on the author's life into English, my main research work at Cambridge being the edtion of the text and its annotation. But I did not feel content with a mere translation, and so I re-examined the whole subject material and consulted scores of MSS. as well as printed works. I consequently reached some new conclusions and introduced a new chapter, along with several new topics, such as, for instance, the mystical life of the author, his relationship with Ibn 'Arabī, a critical list of his works, with comments when necessary and a discussion of his two principal works.

I have referred to Flügel's edition (1893) for the Qur'ānic verses both in the English section and in the Arabic text. I have not always used diacritical marks on common words such as Ayyubid, Mamluk, Wazir (Vizier) qadi (Kadi) etc.

Finally, I hope that I have made, with this study of mine, a further contribution to the history of Islamic culture.

The following system of abbreviation has been used for the works most frequently referred to in the footnotes:

| | |
|---|---|
| *EI | : Encyclopaedia of Islam |
| Ibn Ḥajar | : *Raf' al-Iṣr 'an Quḍāt Miṣr MS.* |
| al-Isnawī | : *Ṭabaqāt al-Shāfi'iyyīn* |
| Ibn Kathīr | : *al-Bidāya wa'l-Nihāya* |
| al-Kutubi | : *Fawāt al-wafāyāt* |
| al-Maqrīzī | : *al-Sulūk* |
| Ibn Rāfi' | : *Tārīkh 'Ulamā' Baghdād* |
| Abū Shāma | : *al-Dhail 'ala 'l-Rauḍatayn* |
| al-Ṣafadī | : *al-Wāfī bi 'l-Wafayāt* |
| al-Subkī | : *Ṭabaqāt al-Shāfi'iyya al-Kubrā* |
| *Tabri'at Ibn Arabi* | : By al-Suyūṭī |
| Ibn Taghrī Bardi | : *al-Nujūm al-Zāhira* |
| al-Yāfi'ī | : *Mir'āt al-Janān* |
| al-Yūnīnī | : *Dhail Mir'āt al-Zamān* |

* In the alphabetical arrangement the Arabic article *al* and *Ibn* and *Abū* have been disregarded. The same method applies to the bibliography given at the end of this Dissertation.

## CHAPTER-I

# LIFE ACCOUNTS

### SOCIO-POLITICAL CONDITIONS OF THE TIME

'Iẓz al-Dīn (577-660A.H./1181-1262 A.D.) lived the earlier part of his life in Syria and the later in Egypt.

Thus he outlived the Ayyubid period, and saw the birth and growth of the Mamluk dynasty.

He was 12 when Sulṭān Ṣalāḥ-al-Dīn (Ṣaladin) died in 589 A.H. An unsettled period of dynastic disputes for power followed his death. This was soon settled largely by the efforts of al-Malik al-'Ādil, who himself came to power in 597/1200, and ruled over both regions of the Ayyubid empire (greater Syria and Egypt) peacefully and successfully. He died in 615/1218. Al-'Ādil had divided the principlaities of Damascus, Palestine, and the Mesopotamian provinces among his sons in his life time, and a a few of his nephews, Saladin's sons were retained as masters of Aleppo, Ḥimṣ, and Ḥamā in Syria. His able son al-Kāmil was his viceroy in the capital of the Empire, Cairo, and he himself, as the head, held the Empire united. But after his death this unity broke up.

Al-Kāmil succeeded his father in Egypt; but his brothers and cousins in Syria and Palestine declared themsevles independent rulers and kings.

Rivalries and petty wars followed. Al-Kāmil, however, exercised a great influence upon the family and maintained, on the whole, a sort of peaceful co-existence with his brothers in Syria. He was the third most powreful and able Sulṭān of the Ayyubid house.

Except for some occasional minor clashes on the northern frontier in Egypt he maintained the policy of peace with the Crusaders. After a firm steady rule of 20 years he died in 635 A.H.

After his death his eldest son, al-Ṣāliḥ Najm al-Dīn, occupied the throne of Egypt. He had to resort to force against his youngest brother in Egypt to come to power. The situation among the members of the family now grew worse in the eastern region of Syria. Fresh rivalries and enmities arose and petty wars followed. Damascus, in particular, was a permanent trouble spot, being continually besieged, captured, lost and reoccupied. Reading the annals of the period one gets the impression of a very chaotic state of affairs in this part of the Arab world.

The indigenous historian Abū Shāma tells us of two sieges of Damascus in less than 10 years (between 626 and 635 A.H.) and describes the appalling conditions in which the people lived. High prices, impoverishment, moral corruption and scarcity of provisions prevailed to such an extent that some people ate corpses and dogs.[1]

On the other hand the Crusaders, stationed in the occupied coastal towns of Syria and Palestine, were keeping a covetous eye on the lost inner lands, sometimes, in fact, benefiting from the dynastic rivalries of those self-made monarchs to renew their attacks. At other times they would assist one king against another, taking advantage of those rivalries, and gain some territory in the bargain. After Najm al-Dīn's succession the situation again deteriorated, and the Franks started new Crusades, the biggest of which was that of St. Louis in 647 A.H.

'Izz al-Dīn watched the unhappy state of affairs with great anxiety. And at last angered by the treacherous alliance of the Sulṭān of Damascus with the Crusaders against his nephew in Egypt, and clashing with him he emigrated from his homeland, Damascus, to Cairo in 638 A.H., as there was no hope for any respectable and constructive life while such a selfish and despotic King ruled the courntry. He had, presumably, much hope in Najm al-Dīn of Egypt, who was steadfast, strong and sincere. He was the last among the four most mighty and successful sulṭāns of this dynasty.

The Ayyubid period ended, however, with the assassination of Tūrān Shāh by the Mamlūk troops in Egypt in 648 A.H., and the new dynasty of of the Mamlūks came to power.

After a precarious period of about ten years their rule was stabilized, and extended to Syria by the mighty Mamlūk King Baybars, who seized power in 658 A.H. He had been two years on the throne when 'Izz al-Dīn died.

In brief, in the later part of his life, 'Izz al-Dīn saw internal struggle for power, wars and instability of rule, and external assaults and invasions. Calmer periods did occur and peace prevailed but only for a short while.

Dynastic feuds and hostilities weakened the Ayyubids, until finally they gave the better ogranized Mamlūks a chance to overthrow them.

The external troubles came first from the renewed Crusades on the Palestinian and Egyptian frontiers. Then came the most formidable menace of the Tartars, who, after shattering Baghdad, marched into Syria, subduing its cities, on their way to Egypt. They were, however, checked and defeated by the Egyptian army in 658 A.H.

'Izz al-Dīn's name was associated with some of those Ayyubid and Mamlūk sovereigns, and with the outstanding events of the time in which he played a remarkable role. Although he was preoccupied in academic activities, he yet spared no opportunity to check or advise those absolute monarchs at crucial moments.

## SOCIAL AND LITERARY ENVIRONMENT

On the whole, a current of probity and earnestness prevailed in society in 'Izz al-Dīn's age. This was because of the example set by the strong, earnest and upright Sulṭān, Ṣalāḥ al-Dīn; an example which was followed later by al-'Ādil, al-Kāmil and other able and steadfast kings of the family. These kings impressed the people with their religious zeal and good conduct, and thus maintained and encouraged a sort of religious consciousness among their subjects. One finds a few exceptions; frivolous and rash kings in Damascus and Cairo who sometimes impressed society with their personalities. Their grip on healthy moral values, however, remained firm. Sincere and pious religious authorities were, in general, highly venerated, and their word had power over both the public and the rulers.

This atmosphere was, naturally, beneficial to the advancement of learning. The Ayyubids were enthusiastic patrons of learning. Ṣalāḥ al-Dīn, though most of his time busy in military campaigns, founded many colleges in the cities of Egypt, Syria and Palestine. This tradition was carried on by his descendants. In the peaceful periods of al-'Ādil, al-Kāmil, al-Ashraf and others, more distinguished colleges were built. Even some ladies of the family such as Saladin's sister, Sitt al-Shām, contributed, materially, to the promotion of education.[2] As the Ayyubids were in general Shāfi'ite and orthodox, this school of law, and the science of Prophetic tradition benefited much from their zealous patronage of learning. Some of them were devoted to knowledge, as will be shown later on.

Some of the kings, particularly the three just mentioned, took great personal interest in the theological issues of the time, and this affected greatly both the learned circles and the public. The sovereigns' favour or disfavour towards a particular doctrine played a remarkable role in religious controversies.

Two great houses demand our attention for their overwhelming literary impact upon the contemporary mind. Both showed a notable academic productivity. First was that of the celebrated scholar Ibn 'Asākir ('Alī) of Damascus, a prodigious writer and his successive descendents. Many of them were eminent scholars in Tradition, and the Shāfiite law. Almost everyone in Damascus owed some debt of gratitude to this magnificent house. The second was the house of Ibn Athīr in Ḥamā (Syria). The three Ibn Athīr brothers wrote on varied subjects of history, religion and literary criticism. They produced works of outstanding merit, which are still valued greatly in their respective fields.[3]

This is just an outline, as further details would take us beyond the limit of our subject.

In the spiritual side of life, a mystical tendency was common among the different classes of society in this period. Al-Ghazzāli's predominant influence in the 5th century A.H. had made mysticism popular among the religious doctors. In the first half of this centruy (7th A.H., 13th A.D.) appeared some most celebrated champions of *taṣawwuf*, Shihāb al-Dīn al-Suhrawardī in Baghdad, Ibn 'Arabī in Damascus, Abū 'l-Ḥasan al-Shādhilī in Egypt. They made a great appeal to contemporary scholars and to the common people. A large number of them with their respective tastes whether for speculative or devotional mysticism, were attracted to them.

'Izz al-Dīn had close personal contact with them, in particulr, with al-Suhrawardī and al-Shādhilī, the founders of those two orders.

Thus he benefited equally from the literary and spiritual authorities of his time. The personal contact with the eminent figures of his age moulded 'Izz al-Din's personality which was independent, distinctive and cogently impressive.[4]

## EARLY LIFE, EDUCATION AND PROFESSION

Abū Muḥammad 'Izz al-Dīn 'Abd al-'Azīz b. 'Abd al-Salām b. Abi 'l-Qāsim b. al-Ḥasan b. Muḥammad b. al-Muhadhdhab al-Sulamī[5] al-Shāfi'ī, called Sulṭān al-'Ulamā was generally known as al-'Izz ibn 'Abd al-Salām.[6] The *nisba* is derived from the well known tribe of Banū Sūlāym, a branch of the Muḍar.[7]

He was born of Maghribi (North West African) ancestry[8] in 577/1181, in Damascus. Almost all original sources are uncertain as to the year of his birth. They state it to be 577 or 578 A.H. However, in the light of his age at his death, which is said to be 83,[9] we can definitely say that he was born in 577 A.H.[10]

He was descended from an insignificant family, and therefore we know nothing of his upbringing and early education. Nevertheless, it is certain that he could not have had any education in his early age, 'being very poor'.[11]

It seems that he was brought up in a pious atmosphere, or was virtuous by nature, and developed an acute religious consciousness in his early youth.

On the subject of his education and virtuous youth there is a very interesting illustration which points to the conclusion we have set forth. 'He was sleeping once in al-Kallāsa[12]. The night was exceptionally chilly. He experienced three wet dreams in that night. Each time he washed himself thoroughly for religious ablution, with the ice-cold or freezing water of the open fountain in the courtyard. As a result, after the third bath he fainted. In the state of faintness he heard a voice asking him: "O! Ibn 'Abd al-Salām, dost thou want learning or good conduct?". He replied: "Learning; for it leads to good conduct." The next-morning when he awoke he acquired the book *al-Tanbīh*[13]. In a short time he had learnt it by heart, then turned to further learning and became, in due time, the greatest scholar of his age'[14].

This clearly shows that he began to educate himself rather late, that is, after puberty.[15] This story, apart from its supernatural texture, points to the fact that 'Izz al-Dīn had a genuine desire, and great esteem for learning, and that he was talented, for he progressed rapidly. Besides, another statement tells us that: 'He was at first very poor and could not start learning until he was well on towards manhood'.[16]

He studied the various subjects of jurisprudence, theology, language and rhetoric etc. under the prominent scholars of his time. The chief of them were al-Ḥāfiẓ al-Qāsim b. al-Ḥāfiẓ al-Kabīr b. 'Asākir (d. 600/1203) for the Ḥadīth, Fakhr al-Dīn b. 'Asākir (d. 620/1223) for law or *fiqh*, Saif al-Dīn al-Āmidī (d. 631/1233) for jurisprudence or *Uṣūl al-fiqh.*

He also attended the lectures of Barakāt al-Khushū'ī and Ibn al-Ḥarastānī. To read 'Ḥadith' he travelled to Baghdad in 597 A.H. where he attended the lectures of 'Umar b. Ṭabarzad and Ḥanbal al-Raṣāfī for a few months.[17]

'Izz al-Dīn had 'a remarkable clarity of vision and keen intelligence'[18]. In a statement of his own he illustrates his mental sharpness and quick powers of learning: 'I never needed to complete the subject I read under any of my teachers. When I reached the middle he would say: "You need my help no more; go on by yourself". The last phrase of this statement: 'in spite of that I never stopped until I had completed the particular subject under him'[19] shows his eagerness and high esteem for his teachers.

'Izz al-Dīn was an accurate judge of his tutors. He has recorded his impressions and admiration of some of them. He was especially attracted to al-Āmidī who was a noted legist and an outstanding rational scholar of his time.[20] Praising him 'Izz al-Dīn says: 'If Islam was challenged by any heretical philosopher no one but al-Āmidī was to be appointed to dispute with him, as he was the most capable person for that.'[21] 'Izz al-Dīn's systematic legal thinking, with its scientific method, was moulded by this teacher. The pupil generously and most gratefully ackhowledges this in these words: 'I learned the method of academic investigation and scientific approach from no one but Saif al-Dīn al-Āmidī.[22]

After the completion of his studies he took up the teaching profession and taught in several colleges in Damascus; among them only one, al-Madrasa al Chazzāliyya, is named.[23]

'Izz al-Dīn was appointed to that noted college in Jumada I, 635 A.H. by al-Malik al-Kāmil, king of Egypt and Syria.[24]

In the meantime he gave legal advice and *fatwās* to people. In due course he gained the public title Muftī al-Shām (i.e. the jurisconsult of Syria) for his ingenuity in matters of law, and ready service to the public.

The *Khiṭāba* (i.e. the post of addressing the public at the Friday mass prayer) at a chief mosque of any Muslim capital city was a respected and influential position at this period. The Umayyad Mosque of Damascus, being one of the oldest great mosques (built in 82 A.H.) enjoyed high regard in the Muslim world. Leading scholars and sometimes eminent qādis were assigned to the post of the *Khiṭāba* in that mosque. Among them, for instance, at the same period was Ibn Khallikān (d. 681 A.H.), the celebrated author and chief qāḍī of Damascus.[25] Considering the importance and influence of this position one might compare it, leaving aside its religious nature, with the office of national guidance in modern terms. But in modern times it has lost this significance altogether.

However, 'Izz al-Dīn was assigned to the *Khiṭāba* of the Umayyad Mosque in Rabī' II, 637/Nov. 1239 by al-Malik al-Ṣāliḥ Ismā'īl, Sulṭān of Damascus. Abū Shāma, recording the appointment in the chronology of that year, remarks: 'On this day the *Khiṭāba* was given to the most meritorious person al-Shaykh al-Faqīh 'Izz al-Dīn b. 'Abd al-Salām[26].

The office, nevertheless, was not held by him for long, as he was dismissed in 638/1240 for criticising the Sulṭān publicly, in a Friday sermon, for his political treachery.[27]

He is also reported by some authors as having been the qāḍī of Damascus.[28] But this information does not stand critical scrutiny. Contemporary annalists like Abū Shāma, Sibṭ Ibn al-Jauzī and other early biographers never mention it. Also Ibn Ṭūlūn in his standard and comprehensiv biographical dictionary of the qadis of Damascus has not included him among them. The earliest hint, in affirmation, on the point, we find in these words of 'Izz al-Dīn's son Sharaf al-Dīn; 'Then al-Malik al-Kāmil entrusted him with the office of qāḍī of Damascus, after he had imposed many conditions on the king and he had accepted them’.[29]

Analysing this statement historically we notice that the said king did not rule Damascus more than two and a half months; that is from 10 Jumādā I, 635 A.H. when he took it, till 22 Rajab of the same year when he died there.[30]

Now, it is likely that al-Kāmil, who respected ‘Izz al-Dīn very much and held him in high esteem[31] might have offered him the office when he held the city for that short period. But after the king's death, when his brother and rival al-Ṣāliḥ Ismā‘īl, who did not like ‘Izz al-Dīn, came to power, he perhaps cancelled the offer. Al-Subkī himself, although he preserves this affirmative statement of ‘Izz al-Dīn's son, does not mention him as qadi of Damascus.

Finally, if this office was supposedly assigned to him, the short duration of the tenure, presumably, made his biographers overlook it.

The case is similar with another assignment: an embassy from Damascus to the Caliphate in Baghdad. The same source, Sharaf al-Dīn, informs us briefly that al-Kāmil also appointed ‘Izz al-Dīn to lead an embassy to Baghdad. But nowhere is it recorded that he actually carried out the mission. Thus again the fact that the job was never done made all the biographers and historians drop the point.

Here we come to the end of ‘Izz al-Dīn's life in Damascus. In fact, it ended on his actual dismissal from the *Khiṭāba* of the Umayyad Mosque.

In 638/1240 al-Ṣāliḥ Ismā‘īl (d. 648/1250) of Damascus, concluding a military alliance with the Crusaders, ceded to them some of the towns and fortifications of Syria. ‘Izz al-Dīn condemned him for his treacherous action. Immediately he was dismissed from the *Khiṭāba*, arrested and imprisoned. However, after a short time he was released on conditions which made him forfeit his freedom of speech and action.[32] He then migrated from Damascus, and set out for Cairo.

On his way to Egypt he passed through Palestine. Here the ruler of al-Karak, al-Malik al-Nāṣir Dāwūd (d. 656/1267) greeted him on his way and invited him pressingly to stay in his small kingdom. ‘Izz al-Dīn was his guest for some time but did not accept his offer to reside there permanently.[33]

He then came to Jerusalem where he was caught up by the same al-Ṣāliḥ Ismā'īl. The King attempted by temptations and threats to win him back to his kingdom, and, on 'Izz al-Dīn's firm refusal of the offer, arrested him again. He was, however, shortly afterwards released during the incidents which followed his arrest.[34]

The biographers and the chroniclers disclose that he was dismissed in 638 A.H. and arrived in Cairo in 639 A.H.[35] Keeping in mind his short stay in those two cities of Palestine, we therefore assume that 'Izz al-Dīn's dismissal in Damascus occurred towards the end of 638 A.H.

He came to Cairo and settled there. Here he was warmly welcomed by Najm al-Dīn Ayyūb (d. 647 A.H.) the Sulṭān of Egypt, and as a token of high regard he was soon offered the *Khiṭāba* of the great mosque of Cairo (Jāmi' 'Amr ibn al-'Āṣ), the first and the most revered mosque in the country. Along with this tenure he was also entrusted with the office of rehabilitating the old and deserted mosques of the new and old cities of Cairo.[36]

After a little while, when a vacancy happened to occur, he was appointed chief qāḍī of old Cairo (called at that time Misr) and upper Egypt. He took over this office on 9 Dhu 'l-Ḥijja 639/21.6.1241.[37]

As qāḍī he was exceptionally strict and inflexible. He never allowed justice and the administration of law to be influenced or hindered by the ruling authorities. There are a number of cases in his short period of 'qāḍīship', which cast light upon this quality of his.

Quṭb al-Dīn al-Yūnīnī quotes Prince Ḥusām al Dīn (al Hadhabānī)[38] 'I had evidence to give on behalf of Sulṭān Najm al-Dīn. The Sulṭān ordered me to deliver the evidence before Shaykh 'Izz al-Dīn who was qāḍī of Egypt at the time. I said: "Your Majesty, he would not accept my witness". But the Sulṭān urged me on. "Then, master, get his permission for me". He sent for his permission, to which 'Izz al-Dīn replied: "I would not accept his evidence". So the matter was suspended till he was replaced by qāḍī Badr al-Dīn al-Sanjārī. I then went to the new qāḍī. He received me at the gate. I delivered the evidence, he accepted it and the matter was finished'. Al-Yūnīnī then comments: 'So Shaykh 'Izz al-Dīn never showed partiality to anyone against the law'.[39]

Two other cases of the kind occurred with the viceroy and the wazīr which made him tender his resignation in protest each time. In one of these cases he even faced, according to al-Subkī, the danger of losing his life. The original source, 'Izz al-Dīn's son says succinctly: "And after a while he resigned from that post of "qāḍīship". But the Sulṭān requested him to remain in the office, and duly succeeded in his request. Then again he resigned. This time he tried discreetly and politely to persuade the Sulṭān to accept his resignation, and he accepted it.[40]

The details of these resignations are preserved in other sources. As they involve legal incidents of outstanding interest, they will be dealt with separately in a relevant chapter.[41] In short, following a clash with the wazir of the kingdom, 'Izz al-Dīn finally resigned on 13 Dhu 'l-Qa'da 640 A.H.[42] Thus he served as chief qāḍī for just one year.

The Sulṭān was compelled by 'Izz al-Dīn, as the previous quotation shows, to accept his resignation, and he regretted it.[43] This is no exaggeration, for Najm al-Dīn indeed loved and admired 'Izz al-Dīn for his personal and professional qualities. But at the same time he was an absolute monarch of a despotic nature[44] and it was too much to expect him to tolerate the uncompromising attitude of the strict qāḍī. This 'Izz al-Dīn perhaps realised, and thought it better to keep away from any further conflict with the Sulṭān or his wazir, with no positive results. So he withdrew from his responsible position and occupied himself completely with academic activities.

Najm al-Dīn, taking advantage of this, also relieved him of his other post of the *Khiṭāba*. This he did because he was advised to dismiss him from this public post; otherwise he would be condemned publicly by 'Izz al-Dīn, as was the fate of the Sulṭān of Damascus.[45]

During his short service as chief qāḍī 'Izz al-Dīn gained an exemplary reputation for his impartial justice. Abū 'l-Ḥusayn al-Jazzār (d. 679 A.H.) a famous poet of the period praises him in a poem thus:

سار عبدالعزيز فی الحكم سيرا    لم يسره سوى ابن عبدالعزيز

عمنا حكمه بعدل وسيط    شامل للورى و لفظ و جيز[46]

(i.e. 'Abd al-Azīz[47] did justice in such a way
As no one except Ibn 'Abd al-Azīz[48] could do

He treated us with impartial justice,
Fair to all, and brief in words).

In the same year (640 A.H.) when 'Izz al-Dīn resigned, Najm al-Dīn had founded a new college, or rather colleges, named after his title al-Ṣāliḥ, al-Madāris al-Ṣāliḥiyya, in Cairo.[49] Now, the Sulṭān, seeing 'Izz al-Dīn's unwillingness in the office of qāḍī offered him the professorship in Shāfi'ite law, which he accepted, and retained until his death.

It seems certain that this appointment took place soon after 'Izz al-Dīn's resignation just mentioned; or so it appears from the manner in which the event is recorded in the various sources. For instance, 'Izz al-Dīn's son's statement:......'then he was appointed professor in.....'[50] We do not know the precise date of this appointment. But al-Maqrīzī's statement: 'In this year (i.e. 652 A.H.) 'Izz al-Dīn b. 'Abd al-Salām taught in al-Ṣāliḥiyya'[51] is obviously misleading, as it suggests that he began to teach there in that year, which is incorrect. For it is well known from various sources cited above that Najm al-Dīn himself appointed 'Izz al-Dīn to the college; and he died in 647 A.H.[52]

Thus Najm al-Dīn, losing him as chief qāḍī, secured his academic services for his kingdom.

A distinctive feature of 'Izz al-Dīn's teaching was the introduction of lectures on the exegesis of the Qur'ān, He was the first to do this in Egypt.[53]

In addition to this he contiuned to give *fatwās*. Before his emigration to Cairo he had acquired a certain reputation in this field. He was also acknowledged as an authority on the subject in Egypt. The prominent scholar of the country al-Ḥāfiẓ al-Mundhirī (d. 656 A.H.) in recognition of his supremacy stopped giving the *fatwās* saying: 'I did give *fatwās* before 'Izz al-Dīn's coming, but now he is the proper authority to be consulted in legal matters.[54]

He also received religious and legal questions from other countries, in reply to which he wrote his decisions and opinions (*fatāwā*). These *responsa prudentium* formed two collections known as *'al-Fatāwā al-Misriyya'*, and *'al-Fatāwā al-Mawṣiliyya'*, the latter being answers to the the questions addressed to him from Mawṣil, Iraq.

Presumably in this quieter period of his life 'Izz al-Dīn compiled most of his works.

In his later years, at about the age of 70 he was present at a battle against the Crusaders in Damietta, Egypt, with al-Malik al-Mu'azzam Tūrān Shāh.[55] Still later (658 A.H.) he gave his courageous and well remembered advice to the King of Egypt at the crucial moment of the Tartars' advance on Cairo.[56]

He taught until his last days in al-Ṣāliḥiyya College[57]; he died on Saturday afternoon, 9 Jumada 660/1262 and was buried on the next Sunday 10 Jumada, according to his son's account.[58]

**DEATH**

The sources differ as to how long he lived. We have two statements on this point. Al-Subkī (V; 102) says: 'He was aged 83 years'. Al-Dhahabī in one place says: 'He lived 82 years[59] and in another discloses: 'In this year (i.e. 660 A.H.) died 'Izz al-Dīn at the age of 83 years'.[60] This difference is probably due to the differing opinions as to his year of birth or vice verse. However, if we prefer the concordant statements of al-Dhahabī and al-Subkī the variance may be ignored. I am therefore inclined to say that he lived to the age of 83.

In this connection, an interesting anecdote is related by al-Subkī, which is as follows:

'It is said that a man came to 'Izz al-Dīn once and said: "I have seen you in my dream reciting:

و كنت كذى رجلين رجل صحيحة ٭ و رجل رمى فيها الزمان فشلت

(i.e. I was like a person having two legs; one perfect, and the other paralised by the mortal blow of destiny). Listening to the verse he kept silent for a moment and then said: "I shall live 83 years because this verse is by Kuthayyar 'Azza,[61] and there is no resemblance between him and myself except our ages. For (this reason): I am a Sunnite, and he was a Shī'īte; I am not small and he was small; I am not a poet and he was; I am Sulamī and he was not; but he lived to that age" (i.e. 83). Then al-Subkī comments: 'And thus, it was as he said.'[62]

He was buried in al-Qarāfa cemetery at the foot of the al-Muqattam Hills (Cairo), with a great ceremonial funeral.

The dignity and honour with which his burial ceremony was carried out was notable. His son Sharaf al-Dīn says: 'Al-Malik, al-Ẓāhir Baybars felt very sorry and mourned him saying: "Alas! his death occcrred in my reign". And he ordered his royal chiefs, personnel and army troops to accompany his corpse to the burial ground. He himself shouldered his coffin and attended the burial'.[63] A contemporary historian al-Mufaḍḍal b. al-Fḍāa'il says: 'King Baybars came down and attended his burial prayer in the parade ground.[64] Al-Yūnīnī (1; 505) adds: 'Nearly all the people attended his funeral; if the Sulṭān's guards had not been there the corpse would not easily have reached the grave, because of the crowd.[65]

The Damascsanes kept their love and respect for 'Izz al-Dīn, which they demonstrated on hearing the news of his death. They called for mourning for him in a mosque, namely, Jami al-Aqība or al-Tauba where a prayer was held for him on 25 Jumādā I, 660 A.H.[66]

The reputation and popularity which 'Izz al-Dīn enjoyed in his lifetime can be realised from the tribute paid to him at his death. Besides the prayer in Damascus just mentioned others likewise were held for him in all the cities and towns of Egypt and Syria as far as the borderlands of the Euphrates, at al-Bīra[67] and al-Raḥba; and later on in Medina, Mecca and also in the Yemen.[68]

Abu 'l-Ḥusayn al-Jazzār, the poet, lamented him in an elegy, the first two verses of which are as follows:[69]

أما الفتاوى فعليها السلام    ند فقد ابن عبدالسلام

رعى الله لفقد امرئ قام    فى الله حق قيـــام

(i.e. It is all over with 'Fatwās',
Since Shaykh Ibn 'Abd al-Salām passed away,
God be with us, for the loss of a man
Who stood for the right truly as one should).

Another poet Ibn Hamdūn al Mālaqī (Ālī b. Aḥmad) of al-Andalus composed a long elegy on his death, which begins:

أمد الحياة كما علمت قصير    و عليك نقاد بها و بصير[70]

## DESCENDANTS

As for his descendants, it has been possible to discover the names of four male children after much investigation.

The oldest was Abū 'Abd Allāh Sharaf al-Dīn Muḥammad, sometimes known as Sharaf al-Dīn b. 'Abd al-Salām (as in al-Ṣafadī's *al-Wafī*).

He was born in 605 A.H. and ḍied in 681 A.H.[71] It was he who compiled a monograph on the life of his father.

The second was Abū Iṣhāq Ibrāhīm (born in 611 A.H. and died in 686 A.H.).[72]

The third was Muhyl al-Dīn 'Abd al-Laṭīf (born in 628 A.H. and died in 695 A.H.)[73]

His fourth son was Yaḥyā.[74] I have not been able to discover any particulars of this last except that he was *Khaṭīb* in al-Tauba Mosque in Damascus.

All others except 'Abd al-Laṭīf were preachers or Imams; and achieved no importance. Only a few lines on them are found in the more comprehensive biographical dictionaries of al-Ṣafadī and Ibn Taghri Bardī. 'Abd al-Latif, on account of his learning, occupied a place in al-Subkī's *'al-Ṭabaqāt al-Kubrā'*. He studied jurisprudence under his father, and the Ḥadīth and other subjects by himself, and compiled a commentary on the Qur'ān.[75]

## NOTES

1. *Al-Dhail 'ala al-Rawḍatayn,* the annals of those years.
2. A glance at al-Nu'amī's *al-Dāris min al-Madāris,* for Syria and al-Maqrīzī's *al-Khiṭaṭ* shows the abundance and prominence of these colleges.
3. Al-Kāmil (history) 9 vols. by 'Alī, *Gharb al-Ḥadīth* by Mubārak, *al-Mathal al-Sā'ir* by Naṣr Allāh, all Ibn Athīr's, are famous. 'Izz al-Dīn directly benefited from the first house.
4. In preparing this background contemporary annals of Abū Shāma, Sibṭ Ibn al-Jawzī and later al-Maqrīzī and Ibn Taghri Bardi's histories have constantly been consulted. Also Kurd 'Alī's *Khiṭaṭ al-Shām* has been referred to for the literary and social aspects of life.
5. Ibn Rāfi', P. 104. In original sources, both old and modern, he is never referred to by his *nisba.* This has been done in some European sources and consequently he has sometimes been confused with the famous mystic al-Sulamī (*Abū* 'Abd al-Raḥmān), see page 49-50
6. There is another scholar known as al-'Izz b. 'Abd al-Salām, whose name is Muḥ. b. Muh. b. 'Abd al-Salam (d. 865 A.H.) (al-Sakhawi, *al-Dau'*. . . .IX; 106). His son Ahmad is known as Ibn 'Abd al-Salām al-Manufī d. 931 A.H. (al-Sakhāwī, II; 181). They must not be confused with our author as has been done by some bibliographers, See page 67.
7. Ibn Athīr, *al-Lubāb,* I; 553

8. Al-Isnawī, Fol. 129 a, Ms. Cambridge.

9. Al-Subki, V. 102

10. This also is preferred by Brockelmann, I; 554

11. Al-Subkī, V. 82.

12. A Madrasa just outside the northern gate of the Umayyad Mosque. It no longer exists. The gate of the building was closed, so that he could not go out for the pbulic hot bath.

13. A standard book on the Shāfi'īte law, by Abū Isḥāq al-Shīrāzī.

14. Al-Subkī, V; 82, see also al-Yāfi'ī, 4; 154.

15. The ceremonial ablution of the whole body is only incumbent upon a Muslim after his puberty, as is well known.

16. Al-Subkī, V; 82.

17. Ibn Rāfi', p. 106, al-Yāfi'ī, IV; 157

18. Ibn Ḥajar, *Raf' al-Iṣr*. Fol. 62 a, Ms. Faiḍ. 1400.

19. Ibn Ḥajar, Fol. 62 a.

20. He was, therefore, disliked by some orthodox Ayyubid kings and finally even persecuted for his interest in, and studies of, rational sciences such as logic, philosophy etc. (Sibṭ Ibn al-Jawzī, Mir'āt al-Zamān, V; II; 691, Abu 'l-Fiḍa, *Tārīkh*, annals 631 A.H.

21. Al-Subki, V; 130

22. Al-Subkī, V; 129

23. Al-Subkī, V; 81'. It was named after al-Ghazzālī and was attached to the Umayyad Mosque, al-Nu'aymī, *al-Daris*, I. 53. The naming of another college, 'al-Shibliyya al-Barrariyya' is a mistake by the editor of *al-Dāris'*. 'Izz al-Dīn 'Abd al-Azīz named in the text among the teachers of this college is some Ḥanafite scholar and later than our author, because the college was for Ḥanafites and the teacher was appointed after the Tartar invasion, when our author was in Egypt. The editor has wrongly completed the name as 'Ibn 'abd al-Salam. in his footnote (al-Dāris, I; 532)

24. Abū Shāma, p. 151

25. Abū Shāma, p. 170.

26. *Al-Dhaiyl*, p. 170

27. For the details see Chapter V.

28. Al-Maghribī ('Abd al-Qādir), *Muḥammad wa 'l-Mar'a* p. 55, al-Nadwī, Bankipur Arabic MSS Catalogue, XVIII; 2. The date of this and the next posts is prior to one just mentioned, but because of their dubious nature they are discussed here.

29. Al-Subkī, V: 100

30. Abū Shāma, p. 166

31. See Chapter V.

32. *Ibid.*

33. cf. Al-Subkī, V; 101.
34. See page 126-seq. below.
35. Abū Shāma, p. 162, al-Maqrīzī, I; 303 etc.
36. Al-Subkī, V; 83 (مصر والقاهرة) meaning the old town, also called al-Fusṭaṭ, after the first Arab Conquest in 1 Century A.H., and the new capital built by the Fatimides in the 3rd century A.H. These two parts were, at the time, under the jurisdiction of two different qāḍīs.
37. Abū Shāma, p. 162, al Maqrīzī, op. cit., I; 308, Sibṭ Ibn Ḥajar, *Akhbār Quḍāt Misr*....Fol. 50 b. Br. Mus. Ms., Add 23, 360. The latter gives the date as 19 Dhu 'l-Qā'da. The difference, however, obviusly is not of much significance, and al-Maqrīzī is much more accurate.
38. He was the most confidential chief and sometime viceroy of Najm al-Dīn, he died in 658 A.H.
39. Al-Yūnīnī, II: 174. The vassal prince presumably was lacking in the required qualities of an acceptable legal witness.
40. Al-Subkī, V; 101. Abū Shāma (p. 172), and al-Kutbī (I; 595) also mention briefly the two resignations.
41. See Chapter V.
42. Ibn Ḥajar, Fol. 62b. For the details see Chapter, V
43. Al-Kutbī, I; 595
44. See Chapter VI
45. Al-Ṣafadī, XIX; Fol. 4b, Ms. Aḥmad III, al-Kutbi, I; 595
46. Al-Subkī, V; 103, Al-Safadī, XIX; 5a
47. 'Izz al-Dīn's first name
48. 'Umar II, the famous Umayyad Caliph (d. 101/720)
49. For the magnificence and detailed description of this college see al-Maqrīzī, *al-Khiṭaṭ*, I; 374. A.S. Tritton also significantly mentions it in his *Materials on Muslim Education in the Middle Ages*, p. 105. For the first time in Egypt, this sulṭān established 4 chairs for four schools of law in this college.
50. Al-Subkī ,V; 81 immediately after referring to his resignation.
51. Al-Maqrīzī, I; 394.
52. It might be a mistake by the copyist, like another on page 474, vol. I: 'al-'Izz died at the age of 62.' Both were overlooked by the editor Dr. Ziyādah.
53. Al-Isnawi, Fol. 129 a, Ibu Shuhba, Fol. 74 a, Ms. Br. Mus. Add. 7356, al-Suyūṭī, Ḥusn....II; 173.
54. Al-Subki, V; 81
58. See Chapter IV
56. See Chapter V
52. Al-Kutbī, I; 595

58. *Iḍāḥ al-Kalām,* Ms. Princetown 1847, (it is unnumbered), also Ibn Rafi, p. 107 An incorrect date, '10 or 11 Jumādā is given by Abū Shāma (p. 216), and al-Yūnīnī (II, 176) Other sources; al-Subkī (V; 102), Ibn Kathīr, (XIII, 236) Brock (I: 554) etc. generally give the day of burial as the date of his death.

59. *Duwal al-Islām,* II; 128

60. Preserved by Ibn Taghrī Bardī, VII; 208

61. The verse is by Kuthayyar 'Azza, the famous early poet.

62. *Al-Ṭabaqāt,* V; 102, also Ibn Ḥujja, *Thamarāt al-Aurāq,* p. 22. All the details about Kuthayyar are accurate, except his age, as his date of birth is unknown. Al-Marzubani, *Mu'jam...* p. 242, however, informs us: 'Kuthayyar lived 81 or 82 years'.

63. *Iḍāḥ al-Kalām,* Ms. op. cit. al-Subkī, V; 102

64. *Al-Nahj al-Sadīd* by him p. 105.

65. See also Abū Shāma, p. 216 Ibn Rāfi', p. 107, Ibn Kathīr, XIII; 266

66. Abū Shāma, p. 216. The date 15 Jumādā' in al-Yūnīnī, I; 505 seems more accurate.

67. Frontier towns of Syria to the extreme north east on the bank of the Euphrates, Yāqūt, *Mu'jam al-Buldān.*

68. Al-Yūnīnī, I; 505

69. Ibn Ḥajar, op. cit. Fol. 62 b, no more traces of this elegy are available, as his *Dīwān* does not exist. The verses are shaky in metre; (the mistake is surely the copyist's.)

70. Al-Maqqarī, *Nafḥ al--Ṭīb,* I; 880. He gives three more verses. I could not find out any particulars about this poet.

71. Al-Ṣafadī, III; 263, Ibn al-Furāt, *Tārīkh,* VII, 256.

72. Al-Ṣafadī, V; Fol. 48 a Ms. Bodeian Arch. Seld. A. 20, his *laqab* in Ibn Taghrī Bardī (*al-Manhal al-Ṣūfī,* p. 7) is 'Izz al-Dīn.

73. Ibn Taghri Bardi, loc. cit. p. 214, al-Subkī V; 131; he wrongly gives his *laqab* as Sharaf al-Dīn.

74. Inscription on the gate of al-Tauba mosque, Damascus. He was 'Imām' in this mosque and reconstructed it.

75. Ḥj. Khalīfa, II; 370, al-Isnawī, Fol. 129a. Izz

CHAPTER—II

# ACADEMIC ACHIEVEMENTS

### A MUJTAHID OF THE TIME

The subjects in which 'Izz al-Dīn took great interest were the Shāfi'ite law and the foundations of law. He excelled in this latter subject and produced original works on it. He was also given to Qur'ānic studies, and in this field, too, he showed his masterly scholarship. But this latter aspect of 'Izz al-Dīn's academic life is rather neglected and his reputation lies chiefly in the field of law.

'Izz al-Dīn was a Shāfi'ite jurist and taught this law most of his life. But he was not a strict and blind adherent of this school. He showed a notable tendency to independent legal thinking, and exercised it, which won for him the title of *Mujtahid* (i.e. independent legal authority). This is attested in the following words by al-Yūnīnī (d. 726 A.H.): و صادر شيخ الدنيا و كان يفتى فى المذاهب الأربعة (i.e He became the master scholar of the world, and gave *fatwās* according to the Four schools of law).[1] Ibn Kathīr (d. 771 A.H.) further says: 'In his later yeras he would not limit himself to one school of Law, his outlook grew wider, and he gave *fatwās* from his own independent reasoning (*ijtihād*).[2]

That he had reached the higher status of *ijtihād* is also confirmed by so scrupulous an authority as al-Dhahabī, who explicitly says: 'He rose to the status of *ijtihād*, and the mastery of the school (i.e. the Shāfi'te) terminated with him.[3] An authority of modern times, Rashīd Riḍa of Egypt, emphasises this further: 'The religious doctors acknowledge for him the right of unlimited *ijtihād*.[4]

Besides, his remarkable work on the foundations of law, entitled قواعد الأحكام فى مصالح لانام is entirely based upon the theory of considering the welfare of people as the main foundation and chief motive of all the laws of the Sharī'a. Considering it a permanent source of law, he set up new derivative laws; while the general tendency of the Shafi'ite school had been unfavourable to this theory of public 'welfare' (*al-Maṣāliḥ*)[5].

However, this does not necessarily imply that he claimed himself to be an independent *mujtahid* or established a new school of law. On the contrary, he remained loyal to his Shāfi'ite school, but did not follow it unquestioningly to the end. A contemporary scholar and a student of his, Ibn Musdī, was more precise in describing him as 'a leading Shāfi'ite jurist who revived the fundamentals of that school, and derived new laws based on these fundamentals.[6]

To judge his academic qualities it seems necessary to find out how he was regarded by his contemporaries, and the opinion held of him by later scholars, in addition to the testimony we shall seek in the works he produced. Here, then, are some quotations from a few of those authorities.

The highest compliment paid to him was by a reputed Malikite jurist Ibn al-Hajib in his words: 'He is more profound in law than al-Ghazzālī'.[7]

Ibn Daqiq al-'Ī, the pre-eminent scholar of the 7-8 century A. H. calls him 'سلطان العلما' (i.e. The Sulṭān of the scholars).[8] This actually became his distinctive title.

Al-Sharīf 'Izz al-Dīn al-Ḥusaynī (d. 695 A.H.) an Egyptian historiographer remarks: 'He was the most outstandingly learned man of his age, and he is so renowned that we hardly need to dilate upon his life and expatiate on his affairs'.[9]

Jamāl al-Dīn al-Ḥaṣirī (d. 636 A.H.) the grand Mufti of the Ḥanafites, addressing the Sulṭān of Damascus, commends him in these words: 'He is a man of such calibre that, were he in India or in the farthest end of the world, you should try to win him as a citizen of your country, so that you could have his blessing and vaunt yourself over all other kings in having him.

One of his great admirers was the author of -Yāfi'ī al-Yamanī (d. 768 A.H.). He begins 'Izz al-Dīn's biography in florid language, loading him with an accumulation of high sounding epithets, then in a moderate and balanced way gives his judgement of 'Izz al-Dīn's academic standing in these words:

'He was among those whose learning, as it is said, was greater than their compilations, not among those whose discernment is inferior to their expression. And his 'place in the intellectual sciences was with the pioneers of the early group.'[11]

And finally, al-Subkī his chief biographer, and a renowned jurist, remarks: 'He was the undisputed leading scholar of his time, well informed of the true and abstruse meanings of the Sharī'a, profoundly conversant with its goals. He saw no one like himself, nor did anyone who knew him see his peer in scholarship'.[12]

Ibn Khaldūn also felt bound to give 'Izz al-Dīn his due credit, along with the very few eminent Shāfi'ite jurists whom he mentioned.[13]

Thus these outstanding scholars and writers unanimously acknowlledge 'Izz al-Dīn's high academic qualities, and legal genius. When we recall the variety of the authors, these words of great esteem cannot be regarded as being dictated by any feeling of partiality. For these writers are not all of the same school of law as he, nor followers of the same doctrine of scholastic theology (*Kalām*). He was a militant Ash'arite, while one of his early admirers, al-Dhahabī, was a *Shāfi'ite* or Traditionalist.

Beside these admiring opinions there are many incidents which throw light on the position he enjoyed in the eyes of people of distinction and of the masses of scholars and kings. We have already seen how a celebrated scholar of Egypt refrained from giving legal decisions in acknowledgement of his supremacy.[14] In dealing with the other aspects of 'Izz al-Dīn's life we shall see more examples of such honour.

Apart from his well known distinction in law he was also distinguished in rhetoric. This side of his learning is comparatively unknown and neglected. Some of his early biographers pass over this point, mentioning briefly' his excellence in Arabic[15] The evidence for the extraordinary qualities of 'Izz al-Dīn in this field might well be noticed in his masterly work on the figurative usages in the Qur'ān.[16]

In his time the doctrinal struggle in theology had long been settled in favour of the Ash'arites and the majority of the Arab world followed the doctrine laid down by al-Ash'arī. But some vigorous Ḥanbalite voices still rose in opposition from time to time, in particular those of them who were much inclined to traditionalism. 'Izz al-Dīn was not only himself an Ash'arite, but also a devoted exponent and zealous defender of that doctrine.[17] The late Dr. Aḥmad Amīn rightly considers him a prominent supporter, in the sixth generation, of Ash'ari's school of theology.[18] He compiled in defence of this doctrine a small treatise which became very popular.[19]

Praising his genius, a contemporary poet, Rashīd al-Dīn al-Fāriqī (d. 689 A.H.) in an interesting verse says:

سما الشيخ عزالدين فى العلم والتقى　　إلى رتبة لم تدن منها الفراقد
فمن لم يجد عرفا لعرف ''قواعد،،　　بناها فمزكوم و إلا فراقد

(i.e. 'Izz al-Dīn rose high in scholarship, and attained to a degree which the constellations could not approach. He who could not enjoy the aroma of the well known 'Qawā'id' (foundatios) he laid down, was either catarrh-ridden or asleep).

The most interesting example of the common applause for his superiority in learning is a proverb which was in vogue in Egypt. Al-Safadi reports: 'And people as a proverb say: ما انت إلامنى العوام و لو كنت ابن عبدالسلام (i.e. You would be but one from the commonality even if you were Ibn 'Abd al-Salām).[6]

## HIS CONCEPT OF THE THEORY OF MAṢLAḤA

Now that we have seen the external evidence for 'Izz al-Dīn's profound scholarship in law it is time to look for internal evidence of the merits claimed for his thought and wroks.

'Izz al-Dīn's genius is to be found not in the substantive law (*furū'*), as is the case with the majority of jurists, but in the thorough and deep understanding of the foundations and motives of the laws of the Sharī'a. One of the general impressions one gains from reading his works is that he was gifted with an exceptional intellect which penetrated to the very heart of things and perceived the inmost factors of the problems without stopping short at outward appearances,or becoming involved in the diverse phases and froms of things. Such was also the impression of a great scholar and religious authority of the 9th century A.H., Ibn Ḥajar, who remarks: 'He possessed the utmost clarity of intellect and an extraordinary intelligence', and again: 'He was extremely keen and profound in apprehending the various subjects of learning'.[23]

This remarkable talent developed, with intensive reading and application to the problems of law, into a comprehensive legal insight. His searching glance penetrates the depths of innumerable laws of the *Sharī'a*, fixedly aims at their essential and central points, and comes out with the basic elements lying beneath the surface; elements which are the prime factors, or work as the current enlivening the uncountable and ever varying injunctions of the whole body of law. Hence comes 'Izz al-Dīn's wholesome treatment of the theory of 'public welfare' (*al-maṣāliḥ*) in law and that peerless work on the fundamental emelments of the laws.

The other impression which is to be gained by looking into his various works is that of his systematic and well classified method of dealing with the subject he chose to write on. More will be said on this point later on. Here we shall attempt to discuss his characteristic and exceptional legal theory of *al-maṣāliḥ* and illustrate it in brief.

This theory is closely connected with the 'all-embracing bases' of law (*al-Qawā'id al-Kulliyya*) which consist of general fundamental legislative theories drafted in short formulae; we may translate them as legal maxims. The number of these legal maxims varies, according to the variant conceptions of legists, from hundreds to tens and finally to the five primary fundamental maxims.[24] These were reduced by Sulṭān al-'Ulamā' 'Izz al-Dīn to one basic foundation, as was observed by al-Suyūṭī[25] and as he himself declares, on which he built his above-mentioned theory. The corner-stone of the Sharī'a in 'Izz al-Dīn's view is the securing of the general welfare, and the avoiding of causes of the evil. This, in fact, is not a new theory put forward by him for the first time. Many Ḥanafite and Mālikite jurists, especially the latter, and indeed the founders of these two schools themselves, (long before his time) had taken it into account, and had derived many laws on its basis. He, then, was not the first to have recourse to that theory. His creativeness lies in the prominence he gave to it and the comprehnsive way in which he treated it. He looked thoroughly at the whole Sharī'a from this view-point, and checked its unrestrained course through myriads of cases and injunctions, original or derived. He pursued this factor so far that he became convinced that the whole Sharī'a was founded upon that essential and all-embracing foundation.

Explaining the ends at which his above-mentioned book aims he says: 'The Sharī'a in its entirety is nothing but a collection of questions of interest (*maṣāliḥ*), either warded off, which implies that they are harmful; or secured which suggests that they are beneficial.

'If you listen to God when he says: "O believers", and contemplate His commandment immediately after that call you will notice either some good he urges you to, or some evil he prohibits you from, or both, urging and prohibiting together.'

He then expresses the general formula in these words: 'And He has explained in His Book the underlying evil of some of the prohibited things so that all evils may be avoided and the underlying good of some of the prescribed things, so that good always may be done'. His positive evidence for this inference is the most comprehensive of those verses in the Qur'ān, which incite to all good and proscribe all evil, which runs:

'Lo, Allāh enjoineth justice and good and to give to Kinsfolk; and forbiddeth wickedness and wrong and oppression. He exhorts you in order that ye may take heed.'[26]

But how can one recognise good or the beneficial and act accordingly, or recognise evil or the harmful and avoid it when there is no specific account or clear definition of them in the reliable sources? Here, the author leads us to a general and practical method of common sense for accomplishing this recognition. He says 'One who pursues the goals of the Sharī'a in prescribing good so as to bring about the beneficial and prescribing evil so as to ward off the harmful, acquires, through his general notion, a firm conviction that certain good must not be neglected, and that certain evil must not be approached even if there is no 'consensus' (*ijmā'*), or ordinance, or ready analogical judgement in the case; because the very comprehension of the 'Law' makes it incumbent upon him. For example, consider a person who lives in close association with some decent and prudent man, and takes careful note of what he likes and dislikes in everything. Now, if he encounters a particular situation, good or bad, about which he does not know the wise man's view, he will still recognise, in the light of what, on the whole, he observed of the other's way of life and customs, with which he has become so familiar, that the sage would have preferred that particular good and avoided that particular evil.'[27]

He further asserts: 'If we follow the intentions of what is contained in the Qur'ān and the Sunna we shall realise that God has prescribed every good, minute or enormous, and has proscribed every evil, minute or enormuos. For the good is another expression for bringing about the beneficial and warding off what is harmful, and evil is another expression for bringing about the harmful and warding off the beneficial. The Qur'ān says: 'and whoso doth good an atom's weight will see it then. And whoso doth ill an atom's weight will see it then'.[28]

This is then the wholesome and independent view which made him surpass his contemporaries, and raised him to the status of *mujtahid.* Undoubtedly, he made himself distinguished by putting forward that theory, with full details and ample illustrations.

With this thoroughness of mind and sharp perception he was in addition free-thinking, realistic and rational in matters of law.

## ON THE QUESTION OF BLIND TAQLID

'Izz al-Dīn's tendency to free-thinking is well portrayed in his emphatic pronouncement that the founders of the schools of law were not the prophets, to disagree with whom is not allowed.[29]. The statements quoted by Ibn Kathīr and others to the effect that 'Izz al-Dīn did not confine himself to one school of law and 'reached the higher status of *ijtihad*[30] actually tend to indicate his independent thought.

An example of this can be seen in 'Izz al-Dīn's view concerning the change from one school of law to another, a controversial point which represents, for the student of Islamic law, the rigidity of many of the legists.

'Is he who follows one of the Imāms (i.e. the four recognised legal leaders) and later on wants to follow another allowed to make such change? This is a controversial subject. The prefereable thing, however, is to take into consideration the circumstances of the case. So, if the school he wants to adopt is one in which a judgemnt may not be annulled he cannot change to a school according to which it must be annulled, as this annulment was only permissible if the judgement was that that decree was void. But if the two decrees were not contradictory then the change of 'school' and the following of the other is permissible, for people continued, from the time of the Prophet's companion until the founding of the 'Four Schools of Law', to follow any legal authorty they happened to find, and none whose opinion had any weight expressed any objecton to that free, varied choice. Were it wrong they would have condemned it. This is a subject about which no sensible person can have any misgiving'.[31]

Continuing, he vigorously criticises those who do not make use of their reason, and remain contented with their rigid thinking, lethargy and blind following (*taqlīd*).

'The curiously odd thing about the 'blind-follwing jurists' (*al-fuquhā' al-Muqallidūn*) is that one of them comes to learn the weak point of his *imām* and can find no defence for his weakness, and yet follows him unquestioningly and ignores the chief criteria of the Book, the Sunna and sound 'analogical deductions' just because he is fond of his 'school' (*madh-hab*) and wants persistently and rigidly to follow his *imām*. He even seeks false excuses to push aside the obvious literal meanings of the Book, and the Sunna, and gives them undue, far-fetched and incorrect interpretations to defend what he follows. I have seen such persons gather together in learned circles, where, if one of them was told of some opinion in his favour on a certain point, he would be extremely satisfied with himself for holding to the right point, and would not trouble to seek evidence for his viewpoint, but simply be satisfied with what happened to be right and to favour his *imām*. This goes to such an extent that he would think that 'truth' was confined to his 'school' only. Such a person is more to be wondered at than his biased admiration for his own 'school'. To argue with this sort of person will only lead to bitterness and the severance of relationships without bearing any fruit. I have not seen one of them give up his *imam's* school when it became evident to him that there was truth in another's 'school' than his own. On the contrary, he continues to follow it, despite its unsoundness and remoteness from the truth. So, it is better not to argue with such people, because if one of them cannot advance sufficient arguments in defence of the school of his *imām*, he will say: "Perhaps my *imām* knew the proof which I do not know". The poor fellow misses the fact that this can be counter-poised, and then his opponent will have in addition the manifest proof and incontestable evidence which the other had put up against him.

'Alas! how many people have been blinded by this type of imitation to the extent of what has just been mentioned. May God lead us to follow the truth wherever it may be, and by whatever mouth it be proclaimed'.[32]

This self-evident and down-right assertion on independent legal thinking hardly needs any comment. Continuing with this principle of following the truth impartially, he disagreed with his own *imām*, al-Shāfi'ī, whenever he found it necessary or preferable to do so.

We find an example of this reasonable principle of 'Izz al-Dīn in the case of a ruler who, though himself an independent legal authority (*mujtahid*), follows another such authority. Al-Shāfi'ī does not permit it, while Abū Ḥanīfa does. 'Izz al-Dīn maintained the latter's view, arguing in his favour thus: 'This, when we hold that every *mujtahid* is right, is obviously plausible'.[33]

Another example we notice in the case of a Caliph or any other respectable dignitary whom an ordinary person claims to have hired to sweep his house, or to take care of his beasts. Al-Shāfi'ī considers this claim legally right, but 'Izz al-Dīn thinks it highly unreasonable and aganist the conspicuous facts.[34] That is, he dismisses this claim.

To this rational outlook we must add his realistic approach to the actual problems of life. His wholesome and profound discernment of the nature and spirit of the *Sharī'a* led him to realistic thinking such as this, by which he gave his judgements and opinions, without its being upheld by theoretical and literal applications. At this point one has to recall his strictness in religious and legal affairs and his keen consciousness of his responsibility towards God, the ultimte lawgiver.

Discussing the various and frequent allowances provided by the Law in all the affairs of life, he gives his own deductive opinion in the following case of practical importance.

'If the only things to be found in some country were those which were unlawful, and none of those things which were lawful were to be found there, it would then be permissible to use what was needed of those unlawful things, and such permission would not be limited to the necessities. (*Ḍarūrāt*). For if it were limited to them it would create a weakness in the community, and consequently Muslim countries might by dominated by idolatrous and hostile nations; and also because the abandonment of arts and crafts and other vocations, which are indispensible for the sustenance of mankind, would not be allowed.'[36]

Besides these qualities, his habit of giving prodigious illustrations to illumine the subjects he discusses is worthy of note. It indicates his amazing mastery of the Substantive law (*furū'*) as well.

In scholastic theological questions 'Izz al-Dīn's logical and realistic approach is also remarkalbe.

Discussing the problem of actions and rewards or punishments he says: 'Some ignorants think that the sufferer will be rewarded for his suffering. This is a complete mistake. The mishaps are not of his producing, directly or indirectly. So, were his child murdered, or his property illegally seized, or he afflicted by some calamity of the body, he would not be repaid for these misfortunes because they were not brought about by him, directly or indirectly. He would be rewarded with the reward of the patient, if he showed patience, or with the reward of the content, were he contented. That is, he would not be rewarded for the distress itself, for it was not the product of his own action. Allāh says: "You shall be requited according to your deeds".[37]

'Besides, the calamities of this world are a punishment for sins, and the punishment cannot oboviously be a reward. The Qur'ān says: "Whatever of misfortune striketh you, it is what your hands have earned."[38] And also the Prophet says: "The sins of believers will be washed away for every disease or injruy they receive, even so trivial a suffering as inquietude of mind (caused by some worry), or the prick of a thorn". An (ostensibly opposite) saying of the Prophet; "Whoso offers condolence to the distressed shall have the same reward as the latter", would be interpreted: he shall have the same reward as the distressed for his forbearance. Such is the interpretation because of the Qur'ānic verse: "Man hath only that for which he maketh effort".[39]

Of 'Izz al-Dīn's logical acuteness and acumen an idea can be formed in the following discussion.

Propounding the relation between sins and various harmful actiosn he says: 'The sin of Damages (*Ḍarar*) is assessed according to the gravity or slightness of the damage done to a person, and according to the degree of the loss of the use or the benefit (or whatever member is damaged). So the sin of amputation differs from homicide, or the doing away with the functionary powers of the limbs. That is the sin of amputating the little and second toe of the foot is not the same as of cutting off the little and ring-finger of the hand, because the assault has made the damaged person miss some worldly and religious uses.[40] It makes no difference whether the criminal performs the amputation himself or through some agent.

'Further, he who kills a dissolute, unjust and tyrannical Muslim is not the same as he who kills a just sovereign, an equitable ruler, or a righteous governor because of the loss of justice, equity and righteousness caused to Muslims by the latter.[41]

The distinction of 'Izz al-Dīn's juristic precepts and discernment of the spirit of the Law, as regards the Substantive Law (*furū'*) can be seen in his *fatwās* (*responsa prudenbium*) and his judical deeisions. They are unfortunatey not published. Al-Subkī cites a few of the author's opinions for their prominence on specific questions, under a special heading alongside 'Izz al-Dīn's biography.[42] The first and most outstanding of them is that he did not consider usury a cardinal sin, finding no reliable sources to affirm such gravity.[43] No eivdence in favour of this extraoridnary opinion is advanced, or rather recorded by al-Subkī, except the rational unlikeliness of such a liability.

In some particular details and situations the question has been, and still is, disputed.44 But in the present case 'Izz al-Dīn's view can be regareded only as a matter of personal opinion. The general Muslim view, was and is, against usury.

Another significant opinion is that, if a murderer repents with the determination of not committing any further murder his repentance is perfect, though he does not surrender himself for punishment. For not to surrender is a fresh crime, different from the former one, for which the conditions of repentance have been fulfilled. This opinion is in sharp discordance with the ruling of the Shāfi'ite school, preserved in al-Māwardī and al-Rāfi'ī's canonic works, which necessitates the surrender of the killer for punishment as an indespensable condition for repentance. Al-Subkī remarks the singularity of 'Izz al-Dīn's opinion, yet considers it more reasonable and fitting, as it gives the remorseful culprit, whose conscience has awakened with a fresh, good determination, an opportunity to benefit from that fair, merciful and humane verdict.[45]

## ON SCHOLASTIC THEOLOGY

In matters of scholastic theology 'Izz al-Dīn was a follower of al-Ash'arī and a notable supporter of this school, as has been previously mentioned. In fact, this school, after the defeat and extinction of its earlier rivals, the Mu'tazilites, represented the standard raional school of Islam. It exercised, and still does, a predominant influence on Muslim religious thought.[46]

In later times the Ash'arite school faced the opposition of the rigidly orthodox school of the Ḥanbalites. The vigour of this Ḥanbalite opposition varied at different periods of Muslim history.

This, however, is not our concern at present. We only want to point out that it was at a time when the Ash'arites were facing such a crisis that 'Izz al-Dīn's significance in scholastic theology, or *Kalām*, came to be greatly noted.

A more orthodox group of the Ḥanbalites had won the favour of the Ayyubid ruler of Damascus, al-Malik al-Ashraf (d. 635 A.H.). This followed their hostility towards the Ash'arites, the overwhelming theological school, and their sincere, or malicious, desire to outdo them. In due course almot all of the Ash'arites of Damascus were overpowered by them, with the support of kingly power[74]. 'Izz al-Dīn, too, was provokd by their putting to him certain theological questions, namely: the nature of the letters and sounds of the volume of the Qur'ān, and the nature of human action. They hoped by this to make him yield to their creed, or else to excite the Sulṭān against him, were he to persist in the Ash'arite doctrine. This actually gave a vital impetus to 'Izz al-Dīn to procalim his creed aloud. He wrote a rather long reply to these questions, with distinctive clarity and in remarkably bold terms. In it he vehemently defended the Ash'arite creed. After some dispute and some fiery correspondence with the antagonistic Sulṭān, and some persecution, he finally came out of the trial triumphantly. This gave him a certain prominence and reputation in the field of *Kalām,* too. His reply became a populr tract, entitled '*Mulḥat al-I'tiqād*[48] (Bon Mot of the creed) and gained for its author a name among the outstanding suppoters of al-Ash'arī. He is reckoned by Aḥmad Amīn in the sixth grade, along with al-Rāzī and al-

Āmidī, who defended and served the cause of the Ash'arite doctrine of creed.[49]

The aforementioned tract is a summary of the Ash'arite doctrine which the author justly claims to be the creed of all Muslims except that small group of rigid and letter-bound Ḥanbalites whom he calls Ḥashwiyya (the stuffed ones). It deals mainly with the nature of the body of the Qur'ān on the lines of *Kalām*; that is, the divine qualities of its inscribed letters and pronounced sounds and words. The tract is excellently written, well argumented, vigorous and readable.

Some later followers of Ibn Ḥanbal developed a rather extreme view of the written letters of the Qur'ān in the existing volume, and of their sounds. They held them to be uncreated, or divinely immortal. For this literalism they were, in condemnation, called al-Ḥashwiyya (the stuffed ones). These were the people who, intoxicated with their temporary power or blinded with their pedantic and shallow thinking, wanted to provoke and put 'Izz al-Dīn on trial. But they received in turn strong criticism from him. He constantly calls them, in that tract, 'unreasonable, ignorant, dullinnovators and anthropomorphists![50] His most rigorous utterance against them was: 'Peril shall be the lot of those who claim the letters pronounced by His creatures or the inscription written by the ink to be the immortal word of God'.[51]

The subject is rather delicate. 'Izz al-Dīn positively holds that the Qur'ān, being the word of God, is a divine attribute of Him, and therefore, is obviously eternal. But it is not that which is read and written by people, because this can be obliterated, and is a function of people, who are undeniably mortal. In the meantime, this read and written thing must be faithfully respected, as it marks the word of God, like all other attributes of Him which denote His being.[52]

This subtle rational concept was feared to lead, indirectly, to the undervaluation of the book of the Qur'ān (*al-muṣḥaf*). In fact, this ostensibly weak point was utilised by his opponents to accuse 'Izz al-Dīn, along with al-Ash'arī, of being disdainful of the text of the Qur'ān. He cleared up this misinterpretation of his opinion by declaring forcefully and definitely his belief in this respect in the following words: 'We (i.e. Ash'arites) hold that any Muslim who shows disrespect to the volume of the Qur'ān, or any part of it, is a blasphemer, and is liable to all the severe legal and religious consequences of blasphemy. That is, his mearriag tie would be broken and his property confiscated, he would be beheaded, would be deprived of the burial ceremonies of washing, shrouding and prayer, and would not be buried in the Muslim cemetary, but would be left for the beasts to feed upon.[53]

Again he declares explicitly: 'Our creed is that the word of God, the Perfect (i.e. the Qur'ān) is eternal, immortal and existing along with His Being; it is unlike the speech of the created as His Being is unlike the being of his creatures. And it is unimaginable that any of his attributes should exist separate from His Being, because, should it be separated from Him, He would become, may He far transcend what the transgressors say, deficient. It is, notwithstanding, inscribed within a volume, preserved in hearts and read by tongues, while God's eternal attribute is neither ink of the inscriber, not sounds of the utterers; and he who believes contrary to this is separated from the faith and led astray from the creed of Muslims. Moreover, only an ignorant and dim-witted person might hold such a view and "Our Lord, the Beneficent is to be implored against what ye utter".[54]

Defending the standard creed of Islam, he took the opportunity to expose those extremist groups of the Ḥanbalites. He classifies them into two main categories: 'Those who openly propagate their unreasonable stuff, deeming that they are on solid and sound ground. These, indeed, are good for nothing. The second group is of those who shield themselves under the pretence of following the early orthodox authorities (al-Salaf), for wordly greed and goals, and play the role of hypocritical pacifists, or moderates. The ideal olthodox path, in fact, is the belief in the divine unity of God, and deanthropomorphism unimpared by any personification and similarisation'. Anthropomorphism in 'Izz al-Dīn's words is the most abominable thing, while the belief in 'pure divine Unity' is the highest good.[55]

It was this denunication of the rigid Ḥanbalites which, (nearly 50 years later,) aroused Ibn Taimiya, a militant critic of all the schools of *Kalām* and somewhat extravagant in literal applications of the canonic texts, to comment on 'Izz al-Dīn. He, however, agreed with our author in his condemnation of the first group of Ḥashwites, who openly applied the human attributes to God, but he refuted 'Izz al-Dīn in the other part of the latter's criticism, defending, or rather interpreting, 'the early orthodox authorities' in his own way, or according to their approach to the theological problems.[56]

The problem of human actions and reward or punishment therefore is of a dual nature, the legal, and theological. It is, however, mainly a topic of the works on theology. 'Izz al-Dīn, nonetheless, discusses the problem in his work on the foundations of the laws. His view of the matter has been represented a little while ago. There the discussion was concerned with the negation of a misconception of the question. Here is, now, the positive treatment of the subject by the author.

Expounding the problem in a very precise and compact style he says: 'A human being is only rewarded or punished for what he 'earns' or does, and this can be eiher by his direct, indirect, immediate, or distant action. For, Allāh says: "Ye only receive the reward of your doing,,[57] nothing shall be reckoned to a man but that for which he hath striven;"[58] "no soul shall labour but for itself".[59] And also because the goal of the religious duties is to glorify God by obeying Him, and avọiding His disobedience, and this is related to a person's own action, as the glorifier of the sacrosanctities does not become sacrilegious because of the sacrilege of some other person, nor does the sacrilegious become a glorifier because of the glorifying of any other person. Similarly, substitution for violations of the religious duties is unthinkable'.[60]

Nevertheless, 'Izz al-Dīn's contribution to *Kalām* must not be exaggerated. Beside the already discussed tract on the creed, he wrote another treatise on the Divine Unity, which, like most of his works, is unpublished.[61] It does not, however, add much to the reputation of its a author in the field of theology.

## THE IMPACT OF HIS SCHOLARSHIP

'Izz al-Dīn significantly influenced his age in the academic as well as in the political and religious fields. His influence in the second two fields is much better known than in the first.

His literary impact upon minds, contemporary and later, can be observed through the study of the lives and works of his students. It would be unprofitable, and in any case, impossible, to attempt to enumerate every instance of this influence, but we shall give a few examples as an illustration.

'Izz al-Dīn's significance in this respect made al-Dhahabī remark و قصده الطلبة من الافاق و تخرج به ائمة (i.e. seekers of learning came to him from distant lands and the leading scholars of the future graduated under him).62 Another early writer, al-Isnawī (d. 772 A.H.), indicates the same thing in these words: 'He was the master scholar of Islam by virtue of his learning...., works and pupils'.[63]

A number of these pupils are mentioned by al-Subkī (V; 80), Ibn Rāfi' (p. 104) and other writers. The most prominent of them were Shaykh al-Islām Taqī al-Dīn b. Daqīq al-'Īd (d. 702 A.H.), al-Qarāfī al-Mālikī (d. 634 A.H.), Abū Shāma al-Maqdisī (d. 665 A.H.), al-Ḥāfiz Ibn Musdī al-Andalūsī (d. 663 A.H.), and Tāj al-Dīn b. Bint al-A'azz (d. 693 A.H.), the chief qāḍī of King Baybars.

The first, Ibn Daqīq al-'Īd was a very close pupil of 'Izz al-Dīn and acquired his learning chiefly from him. In the practical side of life some characteristic featurdes of 'Izz al-Dīn are well reflected in him, particularly in his dealing with the ruling authorities. The same is to be observed in the last one, Ibn Bint al-A'azz. He, as a chief qāḍī, reproduces his master's qualities very vividly.[64]

Nevertheless, at present we are concerned with the purely literary impact of 'Izz al-Dīn on those who came in contact with him, or were influenced by his works later on. Al-Qarāfī, an eminent Mālikite scholar stands as a significant example in this respect. He was closely attached to 'Izz al-Dīn and obtained much of his knowledge from him.[65] 'Izz al-Dīn's literary influence on his mind can be seen vividly in his outstanding work, '*al-Furūq* on the foundationary laws, which is more or less on the same lines as his master's work, *Qawā'id al-Aḥkām*. He seemsto have been inspired by his master, who was a Shāfi'ite, to produce a primary work for his own 'Malikite school'.

This particular branch of law, legal maxims on foundationary laws, was until that time practised only by the Ḥanafite legists. 'Izz al-Dīn was the first of he non-Ḥanafites to attempt the subject, and thus he later on inspired the Malikite scholar, and after him a Ḥanbalite doctor, Ibn Rajab (d. 795 A.H.), to make similar attempts for their schools.[66]

A Ḥanbalite jurist Najm al-Dīn al-Ṭūfī (d. 716 A.H.) seems to be especially impressed by 'Izz al-Dīn's legal theory of 'public welfare'. He wrote a monograph on this particulr subject, in which he in fact overemphasised the 'idea of public welfare' (*al-maṣāliḥ*) as a source of Law, giving it priority over the generally accepted major sources: the Qur'ān, the Sunna, the *ijmā'* and the *qiyās*.[67]

'Izz al-Dīn's theological clash with the Ḥanbalites also shows the influence he exerted upon the minds of contemporary scholars. He turned the tide in favour of the Ash'arites who had been oppressed for some time by the Ḥanbalites of Damascus, and its King who patronized them.[68]

## NOTES

1. *Dhayl Mir'āt al-Zamān*, I; 506
2. *Al-Bidāya*......XIII; 235, also al-Suyūṭī, *Ḥusn*; II; 173
3. *Al-'Ibar* Fol. 286 a. Ms. Bodleian, see also Ibn Kathīr, XIII; 235, al-Ṣafadī, XIX; Fol. 4 a.
4. Footnote, 1, Ibn Qudāmā's *al-Mughnī*, I; II
5. M. Zaid, Lectures on Uṣūl al-Fiqh in the Sharī'a Faculty, Damascus University, (unpublished), page 54.
   For the varying views of some Shāfi'ite authorities on the subject see the article ISTIṢLĀḤ, in EI, suppl. p. 105
6. Ibn Rafi', p. 105.
7. Al-Subkī, V; 81. It is noteworthy that this author died in 646 A.H. 14 years before 'Izz al-Dīn.
8. Al-Subkī, V; 81
9. Ibn Rafi', p. 105.
10. Al-Subkī, V; 95
11. *Mir'āt al-Janān* IV: 153
12. Al-Subkī, V; 80
13. *Muqaddima* p. 244 (Cairo ed. 1322 A.H.)
14. See Chapter I.
15. Al-Dhahabī, op. cit., Fol. 288a, Ibn al-'Imād, *Shadharāt*, V; 301
16. See Chapter, III
17. See page 46 infra.
18. Aḥmad Amīn, *Ẓuhr al-Izlām*, IV; 73
19. See Chapter I.
20. *Qawā'id al-Aḥkam* of 'Izz al-Dīn (title page), Ms. Ẓāhiryya, 4258 Ibn Ḥabīb al-Ḥalabī *Durrat al-Aslak*, Fol. 48 b, Ms. Bodl. Marsh. 223
21. Alluding to his renowned work.
22. *Al-Wāfī*, Vol. 19 Fol. 5a, al-Kutubī, I: 596
23. Ibn Ḥajar, Fol. 62 a, Ms. Faiḍ. 1400

24. For the enumeration and classification of these see al-Suyūṭī, *al-Ashbāh wa'l Naẓā'ir*, p. 75-76. Tibs is an independent science of Islamic Law and unfortunately is entirely ignored in EI. For an excellent modern treatment, historical as well as legal, of the subject see al-Zarqā, *al-Madkhal al-Fiqhī* (Vol. I part 2, pp. 832-1075).
25. Al-Suyūṭī, *al-Ashbāh wa'l Naẓāi'r*, p. 76
26. Qur'ān, XVI; 92
27. For the whole discussion see *Qawā'id al-Aḥkām*, II; 159-160
28. Ibid, II; 160, the verse, XCIX; 7, 8
29. Ḥamza, A.L., *al-Ḥaraka al-Fikriyya*. . . .p. 201
30. See Chpter, II
31. *Qawā'id.*, II; 135
32. *Qawā'id.*, II; 135
33. Ibid. II; 136
34. *Qawā'id.*, II; 136
35. A term of Islamic law, connoting what is indispensible to preserve religion, life, mind, posterity and property. Then follows the 'Needs' (*Ḥājāt*) in the second category of the three-fold requirements of life.
36. *Qawā'id.*, II; 159-160
37. Qur'ān, LII; 16.
38. Qur'ān XLII; 29
39. *Qawā'id.*, I; 115; Verse LIII; 40
40. The difference can be obsevred in the damage money for fingers, see Ibn-Ḥazm, *al-Muḥalla*, X; 737
41. *Qawā'id al-Aḥkām*, I; 110
42. Al-Subkī, V; 103-101
43. Al-Subkī, V; 103
44. In Pakistan, at the moment, this question is continuously being discussed with great controversy, see *Thaqāfat* (an Urdu monthly) vol. X nos. 2, 4.
45. Al-Subkī, V; 104
46. Al-Māturidī's school differs from the Ash'arite in only very minor points, so that often the variation seems only verbal. Also it was confined to the Hanafite school of law, but not exclusively. See Aḥmad Amīn, *Ẓuhr al-Islam* IvV; 91-95.
47. Al-Subkī, V; 90
48. See Chapter, III
49. *Al-'Aqīda*, in al-Subkī, V; 88-90
50. Al-Subki, V; 88, 99
51. Ibid, V; 86
52. Ibid, V; 86

53. Al-Subkī, V; 93
54. This and the former quotation are from his letter, written after the afore-mentioned tract, to al-Malik al-Ashraf, the Sulṭān, al-Subkī, V; 94, The verse, 112, Sura XXI.
55. Al-Subkī, V; 88
56. Abū Zuhra, *Ibn Taimyya,* p. 275. The discussion goes on to the attributes of God and is not related to the question of the body of the Qur'ān with which we are here concerned.
57. Qur'ān, LII, 16.
58. Qur'ān, LIII; 40
59. Qur'ān VI; 164
60. *Qawā'id,* I; 114
61. See Chapter, III
62. Ibn Taghrī Bardī, VII; 208, Ibn Rāfi', p. 106
63. *Ṭabaqāt.* Fol. 129a, Ms. Cambridge.
64. For illustrations of their close resemblance to their master see my work, *al-'Izz ibn 'Abd al-Salam,* pp. 69-71
65. Ibn Farḥūn, *al-Dībāj.,* p. 62.
66. Al-Zarqā', *al-Madkhal al-Fiqhī,* II,; 945
67. His work has been studied and edited under the title *al-Maṣlaḥa fī al-Tashrī' al-Islāmī,* by Muṣṭafā Zaid, printed in Cairo.
68. See this dissertation, Chapter, V

# CHAPTER—III

# WORKS

## SUBJECTS OF HIS INTEREST AND A LIST OF HIS WORKS

'Izz al-Dīn was a distinguished author, as is remarked admiringly by many early authorities.[1] He wrote on the various subjects of exegesis of the Qur'ān, the law, mysticism, and other topics. His academic genius and masterly authorship, however, are manifested chiefly in the fields of the foundationary laws, or motives of law, and the rhetoric of the Qur'ān. On these subjects he produced two works of exceptional quality, which will be discussed shortly. These two are however, by no means, his most voluminous works. 'Izz al-Dīn's largest works are on the Shafi'ite law, but are not original. One of them, al-Jam'bayn al-Ḥāwī wa 'l-Nihāya, incomplete, was of an encyclopaedic nature.

An exhaustive list of his works, extant and lost, follows. Care has been taken to prepare the list in as accurate a form as possible, referring to all the source catalogues of Brockelmann. Examining it, some errors have been corrected which have unavoidably crept into that work of unequalled comprehensiveness. Similarly the accounts of original Arab authors and cataloguers have been examined and some works wrongly ascribed to our author have been pointed out in a separate list with necessary discussions.

New discoveries of Mss. have been added from some recently published and unpublished catalogues. I have mentioned editions and the names of Libraries where Mss. are to be found, only in the case of these last; as for the rest Brockelmann can be easily referred to. When no remark has been made against the title of a work it implies that the work is included in Brockelmann.

It has been considered useful to classify the works by subjects. Brief introductory comments have been made to all important works. These are arranged separately.

## THE LIST

*The Qur'ānic sciences:*

١ - تفسير القرآن

٢ - مجاز القرآن

٣ - فوائد فى تفسير القرآن

٤ - فتوى فى قول النبى انزل القرآن على سبعة احرف

٥ - مختصر مجاز القرآن — Mentioned by al-Subkī (V, 103) only.

*Ḥadīth:*

٦ - مختصر صحيح مسلم — Mentioned by al-Subkī (V; 103) only.

*Theology:*

٧ - كتاب الانواع فى التوحيد و شرحه — Two Mss. Ch. Beatty, 3406 (I, 2) and Zāhiriyya (Damascus) 5207 to be added to Brockelman.

٨ - ملحقة الاعتقاد or العقائد — Two other Mss. Lālā lī (Istanboul) 3701, Ch. Beatty, 3849 (5) to be added to Brockelmann.

٩ - عقيدة العز بن عبدالسلام

*Uṣūl al-Fiqh and the Qawā'id:*

٩ - الامام فى بيان ادلة الاحكام المتعلقة بالملائكة والنبيين والخلق اجمعين — Three Mss. Istanbul University 1197, Ch. Beatty, 3148, (I) to be added to the one mentioned by Brockelmann (Berlin 2304)

١٠ - شرح منتهى السؤال فى علمى الاصول والجدل, — Hj. Khalīfa (II, 1855) and al-Bābānī, *Hadiyya*... (I; 580) only.

١١ - فرائد الفوائد و تعارض الفولين لمجتهد واحد

Printed by first title. The printing has escaped Brockelmann's notice. Thefollowing Mss. to be added to Brockelmann:

١٢ - فواعد الاحكام فى مصالح الأنام or القواعد الكبرى

(Istanbul) Aḥmad III, 1088, another, No. 1089[2] (Damascus) Ẓāhiriyya, 119, another, No. 4258[3] (Baghdad) Auqāf, 7052, Ch. Beatty, 3132

١٣ - القواعد الصغرى

One Ms. Ghota 947 entitled قوله الشريقه should be omitted from Brock., as it is identical with the main work, i.e. القوائد الكبرى another Br. Mss, Suppl. 1203, III should be added to his list.

*The Shāfi'ite Law and Fatwās:*

١٤ - احكام الجهاد و فضائله

١٥ - الجمع بين الحاوى والنهاية

١٦ - رسالة لاجرب فقرسيفقهية من الانبياء

15—Mentioned by al-Subkī only

16. Paris 5291 not mentioned by Brockelmann.

١٧ - الغاية فى اختصار النهاية

١٨ - الفتاوى المصرية

١٩ - الفتاوى الموصلية

Two Mss. Ẓāhiriyya, 6962, 7826 to be added to one mentioned by Brockelmann.

Short monographs

٢٠ - كتاب الصلاة or مقاصد الصلاة

٢١ - كتاب الصوم

٢٢ - مناسک الحج

*The Sīra of the Prophet:*

٢٣ - بداية السوول فى تفضيل الرسول

Short monographs

٢٤ - رسالة فى بيان تفضيل النبى على جميع الانام

٢٥ - غاية السؤول فيما صح من تفضيل الرسول

٢٦ - قصة وفاة النبى عليه السلام

*Taṣawwuf:*

٢٧ - شجرة المعارف والاحوال و صالح الأعمال والاقوال

٢٨ - حل مقاصد الرعاية or مختصر رعاية المحاسبى

The Berlin Ms. 2812 of this work has escaped Brockelmann's notice. A second newly discovered Ms. is Ch. Beatty 3148 (2).

٢٩ - رسالة فى القطب و الأبدال الأربعين

Ḥj. Khalīfa (III, 429) Bābānī, *Hadiyya*... I; 580

*Miscellany:*

٣٠ - بيان احوال الناس يوم القيامة

Al-Subkī (V; 103) and Ḥj. Khalīfa (II, 77)

٣١ - ترغيب اهل الاسلام فى سكنى الشام

2 Mss. Ẓāhiriyya, 4605, 7914 to be added to one in Brockelmann.

٣٢ - الترغيب عن الصلاة الرغائب الموضوعة

Ibn Rāfi'(p. 106) and Ḥj. Khalīfa (IV; 107).

٣٣ - ثلاثة و ثلاثون شعراً فى مدح الكعبة

٣٤ - الفتن و البلاد با والمحن والرزايا و فوائد البلوى

Mentioned by Brockelmann only, (Berlin, 6068).

٣٥ - وصية الشيخ عزالدين

Ẓāhiriyya, 5258

## A SURVEY NOTE ON HIS WORKS

1. A copy of this work mentioned by Brockelmann in 'Dāmād-zādeh 81' is actually by Abū 'Abd al-Raḥmān al-Sulamī, the well known mystic writer, which is referred to, as in the Instanbul Catalogue, by the title, *Tafsīr al-Sulamī* or *Ḥaqā'iq al-Tafsīr,* while 'Izz al-Dīn's work is mentioned (Cairo, Tafsīr; Istanbul, Qilich 'Alī, 43) by the title of 'Tafsīr Ibn 'Abd al-Salām'.

The Cairo Ms., which has been used by me, is a complete commentary in one volume, 232 Fol. On its title page it is stated to be the abridgement of al-Māwardī's *al-Nukat wa al-'Uyūn.*[4].

Ibn Qāḍī Shuhba (*Ṭabaqāt,* Fol. 74 a Ms. Br. Mus. Add. 7356) praising the work describes it as in two volumes: (وله تفسير حسن فى مجلدين) These seem to be two works by 'Izz al-Dīn on the subject, as Qatar's recent library possesses a volume of this work (bought from Turkey) in 300 folios which contains the commentary of only half of the Qur'ān.[5] So, perhaps, it is one portion of that mentioned by Ibn Qāḍī Shuhba.

2. See introduction to the text.

3. In early sources this work is mentioned by the title *'Majāz al-Qur'ān* (Mss. Bankipur, 1373-4 and Br. Mus. 834 bear the same title). The second longish title is that of the printed one and the Istanbul Ms. Salīm Āghā, 1016. This latter is rather a descriptive title, and misleading in its abridged form. As the last word is curtailed the work seems to be of a pure rhetorical kind. In fact in some Arab libraries it has been classified under the subject of rhetoric, which has caused it to remain in obscurity.

Another Ms landberg, Brill, 503 bears the title; اعجاز إلى حقائق الاعجاز (256 pages).[6]

Brockelmann (I, 554) considers them three separate works, (entries 6, 7, 24). But as appears from the bulk of Mss. and the printed one, it is one work. The variation of titles, which misled Brockelmann, is, presumably, due to later naming by the different copyists.

This work was abridged by al-Suyūṭī and entitled مجاز الفرسان إلى مجاز القرآن[7]

7+8. Short treatises.

9. This work is on the 'sources of law' and praised by al-Subkī (V, 103) as being 'an excellent work'. But there is confusion as regards the title as he first mentions a work كتاب الدلائل المتعلقه بالملائكة والنبيين والخلق اجمعين. One line later he mentions another work entitled: الامام فى ادلة الاحكام

The title given in our list is that of the Istanbul and Ch. Beatty Mss. But it is certainly á repetition by al-Subkī, as one Berlin Ms. 4787 bears the title بيان الاحكام المتعلقه بالملائكته والمرسلين و سائر المسلمين and the other Ms. 2304 الامام فى ادلة الاحكام 8 .. الخ. When compared chapter by chapter, they appear to be identical with each other.

10. The main work منتهى السؤل فى علمى الأصول والجدل is by Ibn al-Maliki (d. 664 A. H. ), 'Izz al-Dīn's friend.

11. A tract.

12. Again there is a confusion due to the variant titles of the same work. In early original sources (al-Subkī, V; 103, Ibn Rāfi' p. 106 etc.) it is called. القواعد الكبرى. A few of the Mss. mentioned bear this title. Some other Mss., Cairo, I; 533 and Ẓāhiriyya, 4258 (copy dated 733 A.H.), Mawṣil, 707 bear the titles الفوائد فى مختصر القواعد and الفوائد فى اختصار المقاصد respectively.

Another reason for the confusion in identifying these works is the existence of an abridgement of this mainwork, entitled القواعد الصغرى (in original sources and some Mss. mentioned) by the author himself. Brockelmann (I; 554, 511; 761) mistakenly considers قواعدالاحكام فى مصالح الانام and قواعد الاسلام of Cairo the same as القواعد الصغرى as he has mentioned all three under one entry (2, 2a, 2b). The fact is that قواعد الاحكام فى مصالح الانام is identical with القواعد الكبرى as the respective sizes of the two, as described in catalogues, reveal.

13. This work in addition to two above mentioned titles (No. 12) also bears the title الا مالى فى المصالح والمفاسد as indicated in Brockelmann (I; 554, 51; 767).

14. A short monograph.

15. Al-Subki (V; 103) mentioning this work remarks: 'And I do not think he was able to complete it'.

This was a gigantic plan undertaken by 'Izz al-Dīn to combine two early standard works on the Shāfi'ite law. The first الحاوى فى الفروع is by al-Māwardī (d. 450/1058) in more than twenty volumes (Zarkalī, 5; 146), or in 4 thousand leaves (Yāqūt, Irshād, V; 408). The second

نهاية المطلب is by Imām al-Ḥaramayn al-Juwaynī (d. 478/1085) in 12 volumes.
فى دارية المذهب

No trace of this work is to be found. Had it been completed it would have served as an encyclopaedia for the Shāfi'ite law.

16. The abridgment of Imām al-Ḥaramayn's work just mentioned.

18. A short volume.

22. Another MS. of this work is in 'al-Fātiḥ', but it is in 139 Fol, as described by the cataloguer of microfilmed Mss. in the Arab league Institute, whereas the one in the Escorial, used by us, is only a tract of 6 foll. Either they are separate works or the ascription of the first is a mistake.

26. An excellent work of modderate size (109 Foll) on spiritual knowledge, mystical conditions and moral conduct, based mostly on the Qur'ān and the Prophetic traditions with constant references to them.

27. A concise epitome of al-Ḥārith al-Muḥāsibī's well known work رعاية حقوق الله only the second abridgement as noted by Dr. Margaret Simth,

30-34. Short monographs.

## WORKS WRONGLY ASCRIBED TO THE AUTHOR

Certain works are mistakenly ascribed to 'Izz al-Dīn, in some catalogues of MSS. and printed Arabic works. These mistakes have crept into Brockelmann as well as some other works. Here I produce a carefully checked list of those works to avoid further misunderstanding.

1. حل الرموز و مصابح الكنوز printed together with another mystical work, فتح الرحمن in Cairo, 1317 A.H.

2. لسان الطريقة فى علم الحقيقه الشتهر بالستين مسالة ١٥,printed together with تحفة الاخوان in Cairo,1322.

These two works are ascribed first by Sarkis (*Mu'jam al-Maṭbū'āt*..) to our author, and we then find them mentioned by Brockelmann, in the later edition, (SI; 768, I, 554). He also signalizes a Ms. of it at Rampur, India.[11]

(I) In none of the original sources, including Ḥj, Khalīfa, are these works attributed to 'Izz al-Dīn al-Sulamī.

(II) The first work is ascribed to 'Izz al-Dīn 'Abd al-Salām b. Aḥmad b. Ghānim al-Wā'iẓ al-Maqdisī (d. 678 A.H.) in numerous old and new catallogues of Arabic Mss. and Brockelmann himself mentions 18 copies of it as belonging to this later author.

(III) This mistake has arisen because of the similarity of their titles ('Izz al-Dīn), not the first names. However, the slight difference is misleading, as our author's name is 'Abd al-'Azīz ibn 'Abd al-Salām, while the other's name is 'Abd al-Salām ibn Aḥmad. But two differences in the *shuhra* and *nisba* distinguish them from each other, as the former is often known as Ibn 'Abd al-Salām and the other as Ibn Ghānim; the former's *nisba* is al-Sulamī and the latter's al-Maqdisī. Nevertheless, the similarity of their titles and the addition of 'Ibn' to the latter's name sometimes produced this misunderstanding and, as a result, the incorrect ascription of the works in question. This is precisely the case with the printed editions, as on the title pages the author's name is given as 'Izz al-Dīn Ibn 'Abd al-Salām. The addition of 'Ibn' by the unscholarly publisher, or copyist, misled Sarkīs into ascribing it to our author.

It is astonishing and deplorable to find one modern author relying solely upon the printed editions and consequently ascribing them to our author. He quotes at length from them, and gives 'Izz al-Dīn credit for the authorship of mystical works.[12] Apart from the correct accounts in original sources and catalogues of Mss., his own quotations bear witness to the falsity of his ascription:

(I) In the case of first work حل الرموز a quotation is given concerning a filthy and cynical darwish of Aleppo whom the author of the work defends as a saint.

(II) The style is so condensed as to be almost unintelligible, as was that of Ibn 'Arabī sometimes.

(III) That which argues most against the ascription of this work to 'Izz al-Dīn is the presence of many verses, of a high standard of poetry, the work of the author himself.

Now, it is obvious that none of this agrees with what we know of our scholar, the orthodox 'Izz al-Dīn.

The Bodleian Ms. is the same, but is correctly ascribed to its real author, Ibn Ghānim al-Maqdisī.

The second tract (3 Foll) provides simlar internal evidence. It is written in an ambiguously compact style, and takes the form of questions on *taṣawwuf* and very short answers. One could not expect such a work from the author of *Shajarat al-Ma'ārif,* and the opitomiser of al-Muḥāsibī's standard mystical work, al-*Ri'āya.*

The other 'Izz al-Dīn, a contemporary of our author, was a ṣūfī, a preacher, and also a poet, the author of كشف الا سر ار فى حكم الطبور والازهار a known poetical work.[13]

3. كشف الاسرار فى حكم الطبور والأزهار ascribed to our author only by al-Bābani, *Hadiyyat al-'Ārifīn* (I; 580). It is by 'Izz al-Dīn al-Maqdisī, as just mentioned.

4. مبهج الرائد بالضوابط الفرائد Brock, SI; 768 referring to Ẓāhiriyya Mss. catalogue (1299 A.H.). It is, in fact, by Ibn 'Abd al-Dā'im al-'Asqalānī (d. 831 A.H.) as clearly written on the title page.[14]

5. نهاية الرغبة في آداب الصحبة Brock., SI; 768 referring to Paris 1176, 25. The Ms. in the catalogue is actually ascribed to 'al-Imām al-Sulamī'. The 'Nisba' apparently refers to the mystical author Abu 'Abd al-Raḥmān al-Sulamī, as in old texts 'Izz al-Dīn is never mentioned with the mere *nisba.* Moreover, no other source ascribes it to our author, and Brochelmann himself again (SI; 362) considers it synonymous with al-Sulamī's آداب الصحبة و حسن العشرة . As a confirmation of this, a Ms. by the same title نهاية الرغبة is ascribed to the mystic, al-Sulamī, with his full name, Muḥ. b. al-Ḥusayn b. Mūsā, in Land. Brill, 618.

6. نخبة العربية فى الألفاظ الاجرومية al-Bābānī, op. cit., I; 580.

This work on grammer is actually by Ibn 'Abd al-Salām al-Manūfī (d. 931 A.H.). Al-Bābānī himself in another place (*Hadiyya.*, I; 141) correctly ascribes it to him.

7. مجلس فى ذم الحشيشة Brock., SI; 768, reference: Ms. 1056, 2.

In the catalogue the *nisba* of the author is al-Maqdisī with a question mark after the name....ibn 'Abd al-Salām. This evidently suggests that it is not by our author, and might be by the afore-mentioned 'Izz al-Dīn al-Maqdisī.

8. العماد فى مواريث العباد Ḥabīb al-Zayyāt's catalogue of Mss. in Damascus etc. page 40, also Kaḥḥāla, *Mu'jam al-Mu'allifīn,* V; 249.

This is by some other 'Ibn 'Abd al-Salām as the date of the inscription at the end of the Ms. is 570 A.H. (Fol. 179), that is before our author's birth.

9. كشف الاشكالات Brock., SI; 768, reference, Cario I; 58 (Tafsīr, No. 836)

This is actually an anonymous work and compiled much later.

## A DETAILED OBSERVATION ON HIS TWO OUTSTANDING WORKS

After this exhaustive list of 'I zz al-Dīn's works and brief comments on them it seems necessary to discuss here his two most important works.

1. *Fawā'id al-Aḥkām fi Maṣāliḥ al-Anām*

The work has been printed twice in Cario in two volumes, containing 430 pages. Both prints are commercial, and misprints and errors are not infrequent in them. The one printed in 1934, presumbly the first, is comparatively accurate.

The subject of the works is an exposition of the foundations on which all the laws of the Sharī'a, including religious observances, are based. The theme is that the whole body of the Law tends to provide means for public welfare, in the wider sense of the word. More strictly, the book is concerned with this main foundation or motive of the law. A prominent contemporary legist, Muṣṭāfa al-Zarqā',[15] describing the work as 'an exposition of '*al-qawā'id al-Fiqhiyya al-Kulliyya* gives Principles of law' as an equivalent to the subject, in modern legal terminology.[16] The rendering is not accurate. The *qawā'id*... are actually legal maxims consisting of some fundamental laws, as I have explained elsewhere, different from the *Uṣūl al-Fiqh* (sources and methodology of the Islamic law), which is often rendered by orientalists and English-writing Muslim jurists as principles of Law[17] or Islamic jurisprudence.[18] The subject of *Qawā'id* laterdeveloped into a separate branch of *fiqh*.

Al-Suyūṭī, reckoning the various branches of the law, defines the branch in question thus: 'It is the knowledge of the rules which hold together most of the articles of law, and the bases on which stand the canonic and derived laws. This is the most useful, the most essential and the most thorough branch of the law. And on the merit of it a jurist rises, with subsequent efficiency, to the higher stages of *ijtihād*'. It is truly the science of *Uṣūl al-Fiqh*'.[20]

On the importance of this branch another great Mālikite legist, as-Qarāfī, long before al-Suyūṭī, says: 'These *qawā'id* are of great importance in the law, and of great use. According to his greater or less grasp of them the status of a jurist is determined, and the paths of 'legal decision' (*fatwās*) are opened up to him'.[21]

The work in question is not precisely on these *qawā'id,* enumerating and expounding, or a applying them, as the name suggests. It is, in fact, an attempt to observe a particular '*qā'ida* that is, '*maṣlaḥa*' which lies hidden behind the countless laws of the Sharī'a. He has arranged the material under the main and subdivided topics of the law, and then, discussing the vairous laws, he explains them in a way which shows the wisdom of the legal injunctions, which, in his view, are based on the public welfare. The book is in perfect harmony with his theory of the '*maṣlaḥa*'.[22] It is a masterly attempt to show the said theory in its wider application, not, 'quite an important introduction to the Law' as stated by Professor al-Zarqā'.[23]

As for the historical importance of the work, al-Suyūṭī considers it the first attempt on the subject.[24] This swpeeing generalization is, however, an exaggeration, as the Hanafites preceded 'Izz al-Dīn in compiling works on the '*qawā'id*'. He was, nevertheless, the first non-Hanafite to take up the subject.[25] Al-Suyūṭī's statement could be accurate were it taken to mean that the work is the first attempt on the '*qā'ida* of *maṣlaḥa*', but this is a rather far-fetched interpretation, as his remark is made in the context of the science of *qawācid.*

The work is written in a very systematic manner, in compact, but fluent language, and is easily readable.

2. *Al-Ishāra ila 'l-Ījāz fī Ba'ḍ Anwā' al-Majāz*:

This work is named as *Majāz al-Qur'ān* in old texts. We wish that the printed edition had kept this short and expressive title rather than the longer descriptive one. It was printed in Istanbul in one volume (223 pages) in small and neat type. Although it was published before the previous work on law, it remained unknown, or rather of little repute.

The reason, presumably, was that the author was, and is, much better known as a jurist than as a scholar on Qur'ānic subjects, or as a rhetorician. The title indicates falsely that the work is one on pure rhetoric. It is, undeniably, related to rhetoric, but only as far as it concerns Qur'ānic passages, as it is actually an exposition of the figurative usage s in the Qur'ān Thus the work is more properly to be classified under the Qur'ānic sciences than rhetoric.

Works on this particular subject are very few. The oldest book known, and lately published, is that of Abū 'Ubayda (d. 210 A.H.) entitled '*Majāz al-Qur'ān*'.[26] But it is not, as observed justly by a contemporary writer 'Abd al-Ghānī Ḥasan, on the 'Majāz' in its sense of a term of rhetoric which is actually a later development of the word in the terminology of that science.[27] It is simply a glossary of the Qur'ān.

The only work preceding 'Izz al-Dīn's, however, is *Talkhīṣ al-Bayān fī Majāzāt al-Qur'ān*[28] by al-Sharīf al-Raḍī (d. 406 A.H.), in the scientific sense of 'Majāz' (i.e. the figurative usage).

Ignorance of 'Izz al-Dīn's work was, and is so common that the learned editor of the work of al-Raḍī, in his lengthy and informative introduction (106 pp., of them 70 on the author's life), almost denies the distinction of having written on the subject to anyone except al-Raḍī. He overpraises the said work, *Talkhīṣ*, and declares (p. 30): 'It seems that God wanted al-Raḍī's work to remain unequalled, so that no Arabic book should share this subject with it'. Immediately afterwards (p. 30), quoting Ḥājjī Khalīfa he mentions 'Izz al-Dīn's work, but is sceptical as regards the precise nature of the work, and its survival, even if Ḥājjī Khalīfa's account is true. Finally, in an unscholarly despair he concludes that the work, perhaps, has perished. However, being unwilling to admit even the possibility of anyone's sharing with al-Raḍī, the editor again expresses (p. 31) his doubts as to the existence of 'Izz al-Dīn's compilation, simply because al-Kutubī, the biographer, does not mention it along with the other few works of the author.

I do not wish here to comment on the unscientific way in which the editor has approached the subject. My intentoin, in this brief discussion, is merely to show to what extnet 'Izz al-Dīn's work is unknown to writers on that specific subject, let alone the general reader..

Our author's work not only equals but surpasses that of al-Rāḍī, both in its comprehensiveness, and its elaborate treatment of the subject. The other work (Cairo ed.) comprises 255 pages, in a rather bold type, with frequent short paragraphs, and many blank pages separating the chapters, not to mention the frequent footnotes; while 'Izz al-Dīn's work comprises, as just stated, 223 pages of a (larger size) of neat and much smaller type with no paragraphs or footnotes. It deals also with many elaborations of rhetoric developed after al-Raḍī's time.

I do not wish to minimise the value of al-Raḍī's work. It was, as its author justly claimed an original and creative work on the subject, but, after the publication of 'Izz al-Dīn's work it was no longer pre-eminent or, indeed, fully comprehensive. It is possible that 'Izz al-Dīn followed his example but there is no indication of this.

He was undeniably more thorough than his predecessor, as the science of rhetoric itself had developed significantly in the past two centuries. It is to his credit that he attempted to find examples for the elaborately defined modes of figurative usages, in all their richness and variety, in the Qur'ān. This fine work of his deals, indeed, with the applied rhetoric in the Qur'ān. It is of use not only to those who wish to study the Qur'ān from this particular angle, but also to those who wish to read 'applied' rheoric.

The work was praised long ago by al-Subkī (V; 103) as 'a masterly example of its author's splended scholarship in the Islamic sciences'. Later on, al-Suyūṭī, the celebrated and authoritative writer on the Qur'ānic sciences significantly mentioned the work informing us that he himself had epitomised it[29].

Apart from its importance for pure Qur'ānic and rhetorical studies, the work has also great importance from the juristic standpoint. The subject of the Qur'ān's literal and figurative meaning is one of the principal subjects of the *Uṣūl al-Fiqh* (sources of law), and also of theology. Much depends on the consideration of the literal or figurative meanings of the Qur'ān when a legist derives new laws which have become necessary.

As for the exegesis of the Qur'ān, the 'Ulamā' long ago reckoned rhetoric as one of the 15 sciences necessarily required for an exegete before he could make any attempt on the subject. Later on, al-Suyūṭī classified this subject of figurative usage as a special science of Qur'ānic studies, namely, *'Ilm Ḥaqīqat al-Qur'ān wa Majāzuhū*,[30] to which our author's work is a remarkable contribution.

## NOTES

1. See al-Yūnīnī, II; 172, al-Dhahabī in Ibn Taghrī Bardī's *al-Nujūm*, VII; 205, Ibn Kathir, XIII; 235, Abu 'l-Fidā', *Tārīkh*, III; 215.
2. F. Sayyid, *Fihris al-Makhṭūṭāt*. . . .p. 249
3. Discovered by myself.
4. In 5 volumes, unpublished, al-Zarkalī, 1; 146.
5. Personal inquiry through correspondence.
6. This Ms. is actually anonymous as the title page is lacking. However, the cataloguer, reproducing the copyist's note that its author was a significant person in the Egyptian battle against the Tartars, and buried by the Shafi'is tomb, gives the clue to the supposed author, Izz al-Dīn.
7. Al-Suyūṭī, al-Itqān, II; 43, Ḥj. Khalīfa, II, 1359 (Flugel, IV 577) mentioning the work remarks: 'And al-Suyūṭī could not complete this work'.
8. In Berlin Catalogue the full title is شجرة المعارف و ادلة الاحكام This is actually the combined title for two quite separate works; the first is on Taṣawwuf (see No 27 in our list), and the other is this one. Both had originally longish titles, and in this Ms. they are collected together. This misled Brock into considering it a separate work.
9. Fu'ād Sayyid, op. cit. I; 318.
10. Both are commerical prints.
11. On personal inquiry it appears that it is identical with the printed one, and is in an old catalogue (1928) wrongly ascribed to our author.
12. Maḥmūd R. Salīm, (*Aṣr Salāṭīn al-Mamālik*., 3; 188-195
13. First edited and published by de Sacy, Paris 1821. He has worngly added, with his own suggestion, 'Ibn' to the correct name of the author 'Abd al-Salām b. Ghānim al-Maqdisī.

14. Personal inquiry by correspondence.
15. Professor of Islamic law in the University of Damascus.
16. His work, *al-Madkhal al-Fiqhī,* II; 945.
17. For example, A Rahim's *The Principles of Muhammadan Jurisprudence,* Madras 1911, reprinted, Lahore, 1958.
18. A.A.A. Fyzee, *Outline of Muhammadan Law* p. 20; the title of J. Schacht's The *Origin of Muhammad Jurisprudence,* Oxford 1950.
19. For the literature on this subject see al-Zarqā', op. cit. pp. 939-49
20. *Al-Ashbāh wa 'l-Naẓā'ir al-Naḥwiyya,* p. 4
21. Al-Zarqā', op. cit., II; 945
22. See Chapter, II
23. *Al-Madkhal,* op. cit., II; 945
24. *Al-Ashbāh,* op. cit., Ḥj. Khalīfa II; 135
25. *Al-Madkhal,* loc. cit., II; 945
26. Edited by Fu'ād Sayyid, Cairo, 1954.
27. See his introduction to al-Sharīf al-Raḍī's *Talkhiṣ al-Bayān.,* p. 5.
28. Edited with nine indexes by 'Abd al-Ghanī Ḥasan, and published in Cairo, 1955. It was first published in facamile, in Tehran 1953 by M. al-Mishkāt. Curiously enough its Persian translation by M.B. Sabzwārī was published before the original (in 1951) in Tehran.
29. *Al-Itqān,* II; 43. The epitome is not included in his own list of his works in *Ḥuṣn al-Muhaḍara,* see also Chapter, III
30. *Al-Itqān,* II; 43

* * *

CHAPTER—IV

# AL-SULAMI AND MYSTICISM

## A FOLLOWER OF THE SUHRAWARDĪ ORDER

'Izz al-Dīn was greatly interested in mysticism in addition to his principal subjects of Jurisprudence and Qur'ānic studies. It was the practical merits of mysticism which attracted him, not its speculative or ecstatic aspects, in other words the mysticism of orthodox scholars, throughout Muslim history, such as al-Ḥasan al-Baṣrī, al-Junaid, al-Muḥāsibī[1] and so on. In his own time the speculative and ecstatic appeal of mysticism was strong. Ibn 'Arabī and Ibn al-Fāriḍ were its influential exponents; but neither they nor their doctrine impressed him very much. He sought spiritual perfection and the ideal moral life through mysticism, as evidenced by the particular mystical order *Ṭarīqa* he joined, and the works he produced on the subject[2].

He chose Shihāb al-Dīn al-Suhrawardī[3], the master of the Suhrawardī order, as his spiritual guide, and was invested with the mystical robe (*Khirqa*) by him, and received instruction from him.[4] We do not know when his investiture took place, but al-Suhrawardī came several times to Damascus as an emissary from the Caliphate in Baghdad.[5]

His last visit was in 612 A.H.[6] and it was presumably in that year that 'Izz al-Dīn came in contact with him and received initiation. He was then 35, well versed in the religious sciences and able to benefit soundly and safely from al-Suhrawardī's spiritual training.

After his emigration to Egypt 'Izz al-Dīn met Abu 'l-Ḥasan al-Shādhilī[7] and enjoyed his company. Some authorities even state that he was initiated into the Shādhilī order as well.[8]

Whether 'Izz al-Dīn chose al-Shādhilī for his second spiritual director or not, it is certain that they had close contact and admired each other.[9] This admiration was based on their respective high positions, as one was a celebrated legist of his time, and the other a leading spiritual master. To illustrate this relationship a few quotations may be given.

A group of learned men and Ṣūfīs, among them 'Izz al-Dīn, once met al-Shādhilī at a circle of learning (*Ḥalqa*). They were reading al-Qushayrī's '*Treatise*'. At the request of the gathering al-Shādhilī spoke to illuminate some ambiguous points. 'Izz al-Dīn was so much impressed by his words that, withdrawing himself, he commented: 'Listen to these marvellous words which have just com down from their Lord'.[10]

On the other hand, al-Shādhilī expresses his admiration of him thus: 'There is no more brilliant circle in the subject of Law than that of Shaykh 'Izz al-Dīn.[11]

Al-Shādhilī also conveyed to 'Izz al-Dīn the Prophet's greetings, as it is said, on the former's return from a pilgrimage.[12]

Thus we see his name more often mentioned with that of al-Shādhilī than with that of his actual 'spiritual guide', al-Suhrawardī in earlier days. In fact, he did not have much opportunity to associate with al-Suhrawardī, because the latter lived in Baghdad and died fairly early, in 632 A.H.

## SOME SAINTLY MIRACLES (KARĀMĀT)

This is a subject greatly beloved of and excessively popularised by the writers of hagiographical works. However, there is general agreement in Islam that thaumaturgic gifts are granted to saintly persons, and that miracles (*Karāmāt*) are worked by them. Even a militant orthodox and anti-Ṣūfī authority such as Ibn Taymiya[13] and a philosopher historian such as Ibn Khaldūn[14] acknowledge this fact.[15]

Superficial mystics, however, and many credulous adepts of the different Ṣūfī orders showed a deplorable laxity in exaggerating things.

In our case, the moderate and scrupulous biographers did not ascribe to 'Izz al-Dīn any such miracles. His principal early biographer, al- Subkī, however, records some incidents of this nature, without alluding to them as *Karāmāt*. Later on, in his shorter biographical dictionary he categorically states: 'And many miraculous deeds were done by Shaykh 'Izz al-Dīn.'[16] Thus it was al-Subkī who inspired later writers such as al-Suyūṭī and Ibn Iyās, the historian, and others, to pass on, or rather repeat, such remarks[17] and rerecord such deeds.

Three such miraculous deeds have been usually attributed to 'Izz al-Dīn:

1. 'Abd Allāh al-Balatājī, a friend of 'Izz al-Dīn, and a pious person, once sent him a present which include-some cheese. The cheesepot fell down, broke, and the cheese was soiled. The man bought some more cheese from a non-Muslim shopkeeper. When he brought the present to 'Izz al-Dīn he accepted the other things, but returned the cheese saying: 'O son, what have we to do with this? The hand of the woman who drew the milk for this cheese was unclean, for she had touched the pig.' The man had thought that the Shaykh would not notice the substitution, because nobody had seen him when he bought the cheese.[18]

2. He was present, in Damietta (Egypt), at a battle against the Crusaders. The muslims were nearly defeated because of the strong wind and stormy Nile, when, seeing the difficult situation, 'Izz al-Dīn called loudly several times: 'O wind, (beckoning to it) take them.' The wind turned towards the Franks' ships and as a result they were defeated. At that moment someone cried out: 'Thanks be to God who showed us a person from among the followers of Muḥammad... who is given power over the wind.'[19]

All facts about the battle and the place are historically correct. It took place in 647 A.H. and is remembered in history as St. Louis' Crusade. 'Izz al-Dīn was there with the Ayyūbid King Turānshāh, the winner of the battle. Beyond that, however, the historian does not record any such supernatural event as he is a mere annalist, concerned with facts, not a biographer or a good-hearted bagiographer.

3. This miracle, as interpretated by Ṣūfī writers, is the culmination of the famous case of his auctioning the Turkish slave vassal princes:[21] The chief of them, vexed by the unbearable humiliation, came to 'Izz al-Dīn, holding an unsheathed sword, to kill him. As soon as 'Izz al-Dīn cast a glance at him, the prince's hand became paralysed. The sword fell from his hand and his joints began to tramble.[22]

This last miracle can be rationally interpreted, provided that the whole story is true, as the effect of 'Izz al-Dīn's truthful, daring, and awe-inspiring personality, which struck the prince with such sudden awe that he lost control of himself. Such a thing is not uncommon, but Ṣūfī writers have interpreted it, from their own point of view, as a miracle.[23]

The second instance is recorded in a loose mode of speech (i.e. 'it is said') which obviously implies that it is poorly authenticated. Even if the statement were correct, a sudden change of wind....is not a very unusual thing. It may be that 'Izz al-Dīn, like all devout religious persons, called for divine help at the crucial moment of battle, and, as a heavenly favour, or by mere coincidence, the direction of the wind changed in favour of the Muslim army, whereupon the ordinary enthusiastic muslims took it as a miracle.

The first case is, indeed, of a peculiar nature and a sort of 'unveiling' (i.e. *Kashf*) in mystical terms, but again it is not satisfactorily authenticated and in the later source (i.e. Ibn al-Mulaqqin) is related in the looser manner of 'it is said'.

This sort of unusual occurrence was over-emphasized by hagiographers like al-Yāfi'ī and al-Nabhānī, who have given 'Izz al-Dīn great credit for them.

Finally, we fortunately possess some words on the subject by the man who is credited with these *Karāmāt,* which can be regarded as constituting a final verdict on the matter.

'Izz al-Dīn in enumerating, very methodically, the means of attaining a virtuous character, says: 'The fourth (after reason and the mental faculties) is the supernatural gift of 'unvelling the things that are veiled' (كشف المغيبات) and of using them as the 'breaker of nature' (خرق العادة). This gift is a 'temptation' (فتنة) for the 'Treaders' of the path of virtue or truth. That is, those who adhere to them are cut off, for they avoid their Lord by reason of their adherence to them. Those who turn away from them rise high, for they are engaged with their Lord'.[24]

This is the opinion of almost all orthodox Ṣūfī scholars.[25]

Thus the statements and anecdotes of 'Izz al-Dīn's admirers concerning his *Karāmāt* appear to be imaginary. Obviously, a person who held such a low opinion of miracles as that quoted would not perform them himself.

## ON MYSTIC ASSEMBLIES AND ESTATIC DANCES

This is another matter which appears to disagree with what we know of 'Izz al-Dīn's orthodox views and general earnest character. There are, however, frequent reports, not only by bagiographers, but by numerous scrupulous biographers, of his attending singing assemblies (*samā'*).[26] Because of its disagreement with what we know of 'Izz al-Dīn's personal character, it seems necessary to discuss the matter in some detail.

It was Quṭb al-Dīn al-Yūnīnī (d. 726 A.H.) who first stated:

وكان الشيخ عزالدين مع ماهو عليه من هذه الأوصاف ، عنده رقة حاشية ، و كان يحضر السماع ،
و يرقص و يتواجد

(i.e. 'Izz al-Dīn, notwithstanding these qualities (of piety, strictness etc.) had fine taste. He used to attend the 'singing assemblies', and would dance and experience ecstatic trances)[27] The last sentence concerning his attending *samā'* and dancing in a state of ecstasy is repeated by many subsequent authorities.[28] It is noteworthy that al-Subkī, the most thorough biographer of al-'izz, avoids this matter altogether. On the the other hand, al-Yāfi'ī, a contemporary of his, after repeating the same words (يحضرالسماع و يرقص) emphatically comments: 'This is widely known of him, and abundantly testified to, and has gained such common repute that it cannot be denied.' He uses the example of 'Izz al-Dīn as a weapon aganist other authorities who disagree with the practice of *samā'*.

Another writer, al-'Āmirī of the Yemen, who supplemented Yāfi'ī's work, states in a reserved and moderate tone: 'And in spite of that (strict character) he had a liking for poetry, and possibly attended the 'singing assemblies' of respectable personages, and possibly was caught up by the ecstasy (*wajd*) and dancing thereof.'[29]

One point is worth remarking, namely, that it is only al-Yāfi'ī, himself a Ṣūfī, who represents 'Izz al-Dīn's presumably occasional atten dance at the *samā'* as his regular mystical practice. If we disregard this opinion, it would appear from the earlier original sources which we have cited above that he simply enjoyed listening to poetry and songs occasionally, and that he was sometimes overcome by a sort of ecstasy (*Wajd*). This can be presumed, of course, only if the statements in this connection are accurate.

Nevertheless, al-Yāfi'ī's enthusiastic comment that 'the evidence for the matter is abundant' is misleading and inaccurate. It is, in fact, repetitive, as we have found out in tracing it. But it is repeated by authors of high scholarship, as stated before, a fact which gives the idea considerable weight.

The problem lies in the discord between such statements and the strict character and orthodox outlook of 'Izz al-Dīn. Al-Subkī, it seems, completely overlooked the point. We cannot simply avoid it, or reject the repeated statements made, in affirmation, by more than one early writer. However, my investigation has led to some clarification, as follows.

It is helpful that 'Izz al-Dīn himself discussed the point in detail, and unhesitatingly declared his disapproval of the *samā'*.

Writing, in his celebrated work on the foundations of law, about the grades of the gnostics, he deals with the *samā'*, and classifies it in five grades. The gnostics are also graded downwards in correspondence with these grades. The first grade is that of listening to the Qur'ān; the second that of listening to sermons and admonition; the third that of listening to chanting, military songs and poetry; and the foruth that of listening to musical instruments, the lawfulness of which is controversial, such as the tambourine and reedflute. Commenting on this fourth kind he says: 'If the listener believes it to be unlawful he is an ill-doer as regards his listening, but a well-doer as regards the divine perceptions and emotional states he experiences through it. If he believes that it is lawful, following the religious doctors who maintain so, he falls short of piety by listening to it, but does right as regards the divine perceptions and fine emotional states which he experiences as a result.[30]

The fifth kind of the *samā'* is that which is generally meant by the use of the word in a mystical sense and that with which we are concerned. Speaking of it, he says: 'In the fifth grade are those who attain these perceptions and emotional states by listening to musical instruments which are considered as prohibited by the majority of religious authorities, such as stringed and woodwind instruments. Those who listen to this sort of instruments commit sin by enjoying themselves by prohibited means. Now, if any perceptions, or a state of spiribial emotions relevant to those perceptions befall them it would imply that they have mixed good with evil, gain with loss, well-doing with evil-doing. Besides, if they look at, as well as listen to, the musician, at whom they are not permitted to look, their misfortune and sin is doubled.'[31]

After this definition and elucidation, he gives his judgement thus: 'To sum up, listening to chanting, military songs and poetry is an innovation, but there is no objection to listening to some of them. Nevertheless, listening to forbidden instruments is a wrong committed by ignorant folk, 'blind-immitators' (*muqallids*) and those who disobey God. Were it a supererogatory act, the prophets of God would not have neglected to practise it and to recommend it to their followers and companions. But this is not reported of any of them, nor of any great saint, nor has any divinely revealed Book sanctioned it. Allāh says: "This day have I perfected your religion for you; and completed my favour unto you, and have chosen Islam as the religion for you."[32] Were listening to diverting musical entertainments something of religious importance, God's Prophet would have recommended it, in view of what he says: "By Him in Whose Hand is Muḥammad's life, I have not left anything which may bring you nearer to Paradise and take you farther from Hell unprescribed to you, nor have I left anything which may bring you nearer to Hell and take you away from Paradise unforbidden to you".[33]

This, then, is 'Izz al-Dīn's own opinion on the subject of the *samā'* in its popular meaning. He decidedly considers it unlawful.

He is much more outspoken and severe in condemning the ecstatic mystical dance. 'Dancing and clapping is a trivial and frivolous practice, similar to the frivolity of females; only a flippant person or a false pretender would do it. How could a person who has lost his wits and whose mind has failed him dance rhythmically to music? Besides, the Prophet says: "The best age is mine, then the age of those who come next after them, then of those who come next after them". None of those' who are followed' (religious sauthorities) did anything of the sort. But Satan has overpowered some people, and they think that their ecstasy during the *samā'* is related to God. They are, in fact, liars and false in their words and claims'. He ends the subject by saying: 'One who glorifies God and realises a little of His transcendence cannot be imagined dancing and clapping. Clapping and dancing is the act of an ignorant and foolish person, not of a wise and self-respecting man'.[34]

Thus, in plain and sharp words he criticeses the idea of ecstatic dance and ridicules those who practice it. Now, one is puzzled how to accommodate the sttements of his attending the *samā'*, and dancing in ecstasy with his own sharply contradictory view. It might be said that he changed his opinion afterwards. We cannot be certain of this, as the

However, there seems grain of truth in the biographers' statements. We find an indication of this in a factual account preserved in a fairly early and reliable source. It is worth quoting here in detail.

Ibn 'Aṭā 'Allāh al-Isḥandaranī[35] (d. 709 A.H.) relates in an authoritative manner that: when Abu 'l-Ḥasan al-Shādhilī returned from the pilgrimage, he immediately called on 'Izz al-Dīn and conveyed to him the Prophet's greeting from al-Madīna. 'Izz al-Dīn considered himself too humble to be worthy of such an honour (i.e. he doubted the genuineness of the message). Shortly afterwards he was invited to the *Khānqāh al-Ṣūfiyya*, in Cairo. There also attended with him Muḥyial-Dīn b. Surāqa[36] and Abu 'l-'Alam Yāsīn, one of Ibn 'Arabī's friends. Ibn Surāqa there expressed his appreciation of 'Izz al-Dīn saying: 'O Sir, congratulations to you on what we have heard. Indeed it is a very pleasing thing that there is, in this age, someone to whom the Prophet sends his greetings'. 'May God protect us', 'Izz al-Dīn replied 'O God', Abu 'l-'Alam retorted, 'Expose us, so that the truthful can be distinguished from the untruthful'. Then they beckoned to the singer (*qawwāl*, literally sayer), who was a such a distance that he could not possibly hear what had just passed between them. The first thing he recited (or rather sang) was: كما جرى صدق المحدث والحديث (i.e. the speaker has spoken the truth, and the speech is of what actually happened). 'Pleased with it, Shaikh 'Izz al-Dīn stood up, and the party stood up wih him.'[37]

This is unique positive evidence on the matter, though rather vague. Nevertheless, interpreted according to the terminology of mysticism, it confirms the statement of the biographers in some way. To reconcile this positive witness with 'Izz al-Dīn's own negative view we may say that, presumably, he enjoyed on occasions the third kind of the *samā'* i.e. without musical instruments (more precisely the chanting of mystical poetry), which he defines as 'an unobjectionable innovation'; or at most the fourth kind, i.e. with some specific instruments, 'the lawfulness of which is controversial' and which intensifies the spiritual excitement. This simple fact is perhaps exaggerated by the mystical biographers.

Leaving aside the particular case of 'Izz al-Dīn, the subjec of *samā'* is a controversial one. Many mystic, and some non-mystic orthodox scholars, such as al-Ghazzālī and Ibn Ḥazm, consider it lawful. They have their points of argument, and have been refuted in turn.[38] But it is not the concern of this study at present. Our aim in this discussion is to find out the truth of a matter which seems so discordant with 'Izz al-Dīn's strict orthodox piety, and to harmonise it with his general mode of thought and character. This, perhaps, we have done to some extent, although we must not forget that men are liable simply to change their minds.

## THE IDEAL OF MYSTICISM IN AL-SULAMĪ'S LIFE

'Izz al-Dīn was one of those outstanding religious figures who emphasise both learning and spiritual perfection on mystical lines. In his book on the Law, he puts it in these words: 'The method for the improvement of the heart, to which is bound the probity or iniquity of the body, is to purify it from everything which draws it away from God, and to adorn it with everything which brings it nearer to Him, and ensures His favour. To have good expectations, one must adorn it (the heart) with good sentiments, speech and actions; one must be attentive to Him and present with Him always; one must stand in His presence at every moment and in every condition, as far as possible, but not to the extent of fatigue and weariness. The knowledge of all this is called 'the science of Truth' (*ḥaqīqa*).....However, Truth is not outside the boundary of the Law (*Sharī'a*). On the contrary the Law is full of instructions for improving the heart by means of knowledge and emotions, firm intentions and ideal motives. In fact, the apprehension of the injunctions concerning the outward aspects of life is the knowledge of the manifest features of the Law, and the apprehension of the injunctions concerning the inward aspects of life is the knowledge of its subtle feaures. No one save an infidel or an ignorant man can deny the importance of either of these two things.[39]

This pleasant synthesis of the 'Law and Truth' is the most manifest characteristic of 'Izz al-Dīn's personality. The spirituality of *taṣawwuf* gave a mild touch to his natural strictness of religion and brusqueness of speech for which he was so famous.[40] It also enriched his personality with a tenderness and dignity which overwehlmingly impressed people, and which was the secret of his success in his reformative activities. A modern writer, Dr. Ḥamza, rightly remarks that the mysticism was one of the three main characteristics of 'Izz al-Dīn's dominant personality.[41]

His mystical attitude affected his style of writing as well; hence his delicate and alluring style even when he writes on such austere subjects as law. Evidence for this is found in the prelude and epilogue of *Qawā'id al-Aḥkām*. I give a passage from it in which he personifies his ideal of a godly Muslim. He is speaking about the preference of those who love God for the gains of the next world to the gains of his world, in the course of a discussion on causes of good and things conducive to it, and he says in a decorative style:

'Glorified be He who makes Himself known to thee without any toil and strain, or proof-seeking and exertion on their part. He showers them with His generosity, and offers them a 'drink' from His pure 'downpour' and sheer favour; and thus He attracts them to himself alone, alienating them from all other things. Thus they have no concern but Him, no intimate but Him no one on whom to depend but Him, for they know well that there is no refuge in anyone, and no recourse to anyone but Him. So they are content with His decree, bear the tribulations which He sends and thank Him for His grace. They are made happy by that which grieves others, and are grieved by that which makes others happy. Their culture is the Qur'ān, their tutor is The All-Compassionate, their companion is The Omnipotent, and their garb is Obedience. They cut themselves off from their fellow men and emigrate from their lands to His realm. Their weeping is constant, and their joy is brief.'[42]

Glimpses of this ideal spirituality are found in 'Izz al-Dīn's personality.[43]

Al-Subkī, pointing to 'Izz al-Dīn's significance in mysticism remarks: 'He was well versed in mysticism, and his works on the subject sufficiently prove this hypothesis.[44]

'Izz al-Dīn wrote two main works on the subject of mysticism, which I have already mentioned in the list of his works. These are extant but unpublished and not well known. Two other published works, with which a modern writer of al-Azhar has credited him, are falsely attributed to him.[45]

However, 'Izz al-Dīn's contribution to mysticism is of secondary importance. The main field of his literary productivity was the law and Qur'ānic studies, as stated before. The mystical side of his life, however, has been rather neglected, and it is hoped that the present study has shed some light on it.

## RELATION WITH IBN AL-'ARABI

The great mystic Muḥyī al-Dīn Ibn 'Arabi (d. 638/1240) was a contemporary of 'Izz al-Dīn. It is certain that they were associated, although the nature of the association is unknown. We are told by al-Dhahabī in the usual way in which the authenticity of a tradition is established (i.e. by following it back through the chain of its transmitters: himself - Ibn Taimiya - Tāj al-Dīn al-Fizārī)[49] that 'Izz al-Dīn used to borrow Ibn Ḥazm's work *al-Muḥallā*[47] from Ibn 'Arabī[48].

Another authority, 'Abd al-Ghaffār b. Nūḥ al-Qūṣī[47] informs us-by way of direct reliable sources - that' 'Izz al-Dīn was once with Ibn 'Arabī' in the latter's room, where an incident predicted by means of *kashf* took place.[50]

This fairly indicates their association. However, we never come across Ibn 'Arabī's name mentioned in 'Izz al-Dīn's biography; the latter, on the other hand, is cited, in numerous works criticising or defending Ibn 'Arabī, by the rival groups of orthodox scholars and pro-Ibn 'Arabī Ṣūfī writers, respectively. It is noteworthy that both of the groups seem very eager to quote 'Izz al-Dīn to strengthen their conflicting views.

Indeed, there is a remarkable difference between the two personalities, and only a slight common interest, Ibn 'Arabī was a mystic philosopher and subscribed to a monistic doctrine;[51] 'Izz al-Dīn, as is well known, was an orthodox scholar - jurist. His attitude to Ṣūfīsm was that of early orthodox Ṣūfī masters He regarded it as a means to purify the spirit and to promote piety, in agreement with the 'Sunnah' of the holy prophet. Yet, because there are such cnotradictory statements attributed to him concerning Ibn 'Arabī it is necessary to investigate the matter, as far as possible in the present circumstances, and to discuss the subject in some detail.

Before representing 'Izz al-Dīn's view of him we must recall that Ibn 'Arabī is one of the figures of great controversy in the history of Islam. From the beginning, people were divided into three groups in their attitudes towards his teachings:

1. Traditionalists, in general, who opposed and criticised him bitterly; Ibn Taimiya was the chief among them. He emphatically and repeatedly denounces him as a heretic.

2. Scholar-jurists (*fuqahā*) and Ṣūfī writers who favoured and admired him highly, such as Qāḍī al-Zamalkānī (d. 651 A.H.) and later on al-Firūzābādī, al-Suyūṭī, al-Sha'rānī etc., and prior to them our author, 'In his later days'.[52]

3. Moderate scholars, who reserved their judgement on him, such as al-Yāfi'ī, Ibn Kathīr and many others, up to the present day.[53]

To begin with 'Izz al-Dīn's denunciation of Ibn 'Arabī, he is reported as saying of him: شيخ سوء كذاب يقول بقدم العالم ولا يحرم فرجا (i.e. He is an evil disposed person and a liar; he maintains the eternity of the world and does not consider adultery to be prohibited).[54]

This is indeed a striking denunciation, and one which, in fact, created a problem for me, and was the starting point for my investigation of the relations of those two distinguished contemporaries. In the light of their association, as portrayed in the foregoing passages, I began to doubt that 'Izz al-Dīn had written these severe words, and I attempted to examine them historically and analytically.

The authorities who record this saying are Ibn Taymiya, al-Dhahabī, and al-Ṣafadī. They are contemporaries, Ibn Taymiya being the senior, and independent in their transmission. The final link in the chain of authorites going back to the speaker is Ibn Daqīq al-'Īd (d. 702 A.H.), an admirable student of 'Izz al-Dīn, from Egypt.[55]

We note, referring to these sources, that the remark is transmitted in a very careful manner, particularly by al-Ṣafadī. He copies it from the writing of Ibn Sayyid al-Nās[56] (d. 734 A.H.) who had it direct from the final authority: Ibn Daqīq al-'Īd, his master. This leaves scarcely any doubt as to its authenticity.

Now, this condemnation, set against the fact of 'Izz al-Dīn's borrowing books from Ibn 'Arabī as stated before, makes the position rather difficult. We cannot imagine that a person who borrowed books from another would hold such a low opinion of him. There is another point to be noted: al-Fizārī's statement that he fetched books from Ibn 'Arabī for his master, 'Izz al-Dīn, is earlier in date than that of Ibn Daqīq al-'Īd, the central point of the problem. The latter met 'Izz al-Dīn after his emigration to Cairo in 639 A.H. Moreover, Ibn Taymiya's version of the denunciation indicates clearly that 'Izz al-Dīn uttered it when asked his opinion of Ibn 'Arabī on arriving at Cairo.[57] This means that 'Izz al-Dīn changed his opinion of Ibn 'Arabī in Cairo, which is not very plausible, in the light of the argument which follows.

There is another way to take this short, sharp ad ambiguous remark of 'Izz al-Dīn. Reading those words together with the remaining part of 'Izz al-Dīn's speech illuminates the whole subject and solves the problem.

The first man who heard (i.e. Ibn Daqīq al-'Īd) this mysterious and cruel remark was shocked and in turn asked: 'And what is his (i.e. Ibn 'Arabi's) lie?' 'He', replied 'Izz al-Dīn, 'maintains that human beings cannot marry the Jinn, because a Jinni is a subtle spirit and a human being a concrete being, so that they cannot be united! Later he claims that he married a woman from the jinnfolk. She stayed with him for some time. Afterwards they quarrelled; she hit him with a camelbone and injured him. He showed us the scar on his face.[58]

This, then, is the explanation of Ibn 'Arabī's lie, and his 'not considering adultery to be prohibited', for he maintained the unlawfulness of marriage between human beings and the jinn, and at the same time himself claimed to be married to a woman of the jinn.

As for the third allegation ('he maintains the eternity of the world') we find that too illustrated in the same statement of 'Izz al-Dīn, which continues as follows: 'Ibn al-'Arabī[59] and Ibn Surāqa[60] passed through the 'Frādīs gate'[61], whereas Ibn al-'Arabī said that after so and so many thousand years he and Ibn Surāqa would pass through that gate in the very same manner'.[62]

In the light of this peculiar claim of Ibn 'Arabī 'Izz al-Dīn's critical remark appears natural and reasonable, although the severity of his words cannot be denied. However, it was unjust on the part of Ibn Taymiya and al-Dhahabī to misrepresent 'Izz al-Dīn's view (i.e. cut off from its context), which as we saw was a comment on a particular unreasonable calim of Ibn 'Aarbī.

It seems that this remark of 'Izz al-Dīn's was quite well known, as some Ṣūfī writers also record it. 'Al-Yāfi'ī (d. 768 A.H.) in his book *al-Irshād* says: 'I heard that Shaykh 'Izz al-Dīn used to vilify Ibn al-'Arabī, and said that he was a *zindīq* (i.e. heretic).[63] Abd al-Ra'ūf al-Munāwī, a staunch adherent of Ibn 'Arabī,[64] says much the same.

The other extremist group of Ṣūfī scholars not only categorically deny that 'Izz al-Dīn made any such denunciation of Ibn 'Arabī, but even represent him as a great admirer of Ibn Arabī.

Al-Fīrūzābādī, the author of al-Qāmūs (d. 817 A.H.) refuting Ibn al-Khayyāṭ al-Yamanī[65], a critic of Ibn 'Arabī, says: 'His citation of the opinion of 'Izz al-Dīn against Ibn 'Arabī is incorrect, or rather, a lie and falsehood for we have been told by...' He then relates an interesting story on the authority of an attendant and student of 'Izz al-Dīn: Once, at one of 'Izz al-Dīn's lectures on law they came across the word *zindīq*. A linguistic question was raised as to the origin of it. When one of the audience replied that it was a word of Persian origin, meaning: 'One who conceals his disbelief and simulates belief', someone asked: 'Who, for example?' Another student replied: 'Ibn 'Arabī, in Damascus'. 'Izz al-Dīn did not speak, nor did he comment on this exemplification. Later the same day, at dinner, the attendant asked him: 'Who is the *quṭb* (i.e. hierarch of the saints) in our days?' He first tried to ignore the question, and then, as the questioner persisted, said smiling: 'Shaikh Muḥyi al-Dīn Ibn 'Arabī'. The man was bewildered, and argued: 'At the lecture a severe remark was passed on him and you kept silent'. 'Be silent; That was a gatherling of the canonists (*fuqahā'*)[66], said 'Izz al-Dīn.

All-Sha'rānī (d. 973 A.H.), who also relates this story, puts into 'Izz al-Dīn's mouth as a defence of Ibn 'Arabī in these words: 'Some of the religious doctors condemn him, in sympathy with the mediocre canonists who cannot grasp thoroughly the divine mental condition of the saints (i.e. *fuqarā'*). They fear that, otherwise, such rigid persons would, perhaps, understand the Shaykh in a way which is contradictory to the Sharī'a (canonical doctrine), and thus would go astray. If they had mixed with the *fuqarā* they would have learned their terminology and would have escaped the risk of breaking the Sharī'a'.[67]

This apologetic statement seems to accord well with the above-quoted words of 'Izz al-Dīn. But it is lacking in authentification, for al-Sha'rānī gives no source, and it is, therefore, doubtful.

The same author also quotes al-Fīrūzābādī in Ibn 'Arabī's defence: 'The rumour that has been spread by some of our opponents, that Shaykh 'Izz al-Dīn and our master Sirāj al-Dīn al-Bulqinī advised the burning of his books, is a lie. If they had been burnt, no copy of them would have survived in Syria and Egypt, and no one would have transcribed them after the condemnation of these two authorities'.[68]

The argument is evidently not a strong one. However, we find in no other source a mention of 'Izz al-Dīn's giving such advice.

In the third group are those who admit that 'Izz al-Dīn condemned Ibn 'Arabī as a heretic, but state that he later changed his view to the other extreme, and considered him to be the holiest of saints. All-Yāfi'ī, admitting the fact of Ibn 'Arabī's being condemned by 'Izz al-Dīn, relates the same 'story of the *quṭb*', but his story is quite different in its details from the one cited before. Here 'some companion of 'Izz al-Dīn' asks him to show him the *quṭb*. 'Izz al-Dīn points to Ibn 'Arabī saying: 'He is there'. Being asked 'Do you not denounce him?' he gives an explanation: 'I keep the exoteric teaching of the Sharī'a'. To vouch for the authenticity of the story the author, al-Yāfi'ī, says: 'I was informed of it by numerous reliable persons of Egyipt and Syria'[69]

The same anecdote of the *Quṭb* he again copies from the mystic-'Abd al-Ghaffār[70] (d. 708 A.H.). There is a slight difference in details this time, but it is more precise. Here the scene is the great Mosque of Damascus. 'Izz al-Dīn enters the mosque with his attendant. The attendant reminds him of his promise to show him the *quṭb*. He, in answer, points to Ibn 'Arabī, who is sitting among a crowd of people: 'That is He'. The amazed attendant asks: 'Sir, in spite of what you say against him?' The master repeats his words again and again.[71]

In this version there is no explanation of his contradictory view by 'Izz al-Dīn himself.

We find the original transmitter 'Abd al-Ghaffār trying to solve the problem. He comments: 'If he was the holiest of saints it does mean that there is a paradox in Shaykh 'Izz al-Dīn's opinion about him, because the Shaykh judged him in the light of his outward actions and works, in keeping with canonic doctrine. Secret beliefs and intentions are the responsibility of God, who will deal with them as He likes. It is possible that Shaykh 'Izz al-Dīn happened to realise Ibn 'Arabī's high spiritual rank and could not deny it. But when some opinion contrary to the canonical doctrines was expressed by him, 'Izz al-Dīn condemned him in order to keep firm the hearts of the shallow ones, and to abide by the exoteric teachings of the Sharī'a, which he was bound to. Thus he gave to each of the cases its due consideration.[72]

Al-Suyūṭī realises the incongruity of 'Izz al-Dīn's opinion concerning Ibn 'Arabī, for he says specifically: 'Izz al-Dīn held two views of him. On the one hand he vilified him, and on the other he described him as the holiest of saints.[73] In fact, he cited the story just quoted and 'Abd al-Ghaffār's comment to reconcile these contradictory views, but he was not satisfied with this attempt at reconciling them, and cites another such attempt by Tāj al-Dīn b. 'Aṭā' Allāh (al-Iskandarāni d. 709 A.H.) from his book *Laṭā'if al-Minan*: 'Izz al-Dīn, in his earlier days, was preoccupied, like the other scholar-Jurists, with denouncing the mystics. But when Abu al-Ḥasan al-Shādhilī, returning from his pilgrimage, conveyed to him greetings from the Prophet, from then on he yielded to mysticism; chose the company of al-Shādhilī and began to overpraise the mystics, as he now understood their ways'.[74] And on this statement al-Suyūṭī comments: 'The reconciliation brought about by Ibn 'Aṭā' aAllāh is preferable'.[75]

This solution on chronological lines seems, at first glance, convincing, and it actually did satisfy some later Ṣūfī writers as al-Sha'rānī,[76] al-Munāwī[77] and a contemporary scholar Dr. al-Munajjid,[78] who takes the same view.

This solution is, however, quite improbable, because:

1. Al-Suyūṭī's source, Ibn Aṭā' Allāh, says nothing about 'Izz al-Dīn's first denouncing the mystics and then over-praising them. The case of al-Shādhilī's meeting and 'greetings' is mentioned there,[79] but no attempt is made by the author to reconcile 'Izz al-Dīn's conflicting views.

2. Al-Shādhilī was not from the same school of monoistic mystics as was Ibn 'Arabī. On the contrary, his able successor al-Mursī is cited against Ibn 'Arabī by his bitter critic Ibn Taymiya.[80]

3. 'Izz al-Dīn met al-Shādhilī in Cairo after the death of Ibn 'Arabī (638 A.H.) and those who attribute to him the words describing Ibn 'Arābī as the *quṭb* mean that he did so during the lifetime of Ibn 'Arabī. So, if this attribution is correct it must be before 'Izz al-Dīn's meeting with al-Shādhilī.

To the same criticism is subject another such attempt of reconciliation, this time by al-Sha'rānī who, on his own behalf, says: 'After his (i.e.

'Izz al-Dīn's) accompanying al-Shādhilī, he began to attribute to him the high qualities of saintship, gnosis and 'Poleship'[81] (الولاية و العرفان والقطبية).

Thus the solution on a chronological basis, offered by these two authorities, does not help and is historically incorrect. At this point we also recall that 'Izz al-Dīn's unfavourable opinion of Ibn 'Arabī was expressed in Cairo — that is, after the death of Ibn 'Arabī.

After the exposition and analytical examination of these conflicting statements on the subject we conclude that both the orthodox scholars and Ṣūfī or pro-Ibn 'Arabī writers were driven by their respective conflicting tendencies. They saw the matter from one point of view and ignored the other. No attempt was made by any of them to discover the relationship between the two great contemporaries, so that 'Izz al-Dīn's opinion of Ibn 'Arabī could be scientifically weighed. To quote 'Izz al-Dīn for their judgement for or against Ibn 'Arabī was not a proper way to show their relationship. It was more irresponsible on the part of Ibn 'Arabī's sentimental admirers and defenders, who related curious and inaccurate stories to support their view. We recall, for example, the 'story of the *quṭb'*, which is once said to have taken place in Cairo, and another time in Damascus; this disagreement is both confusing and significant.

In our opinion, 'Izz al-Dīn did not give a considered judgement of Ibn 'Arabī. He knew and met him, but they did not come into close contact because the subjects in which they were interested were quite unrelated; and also, in mysticism, 'Izz al-Dīn preferred, from his earliest days, the orthodox 'path' (*ṭarīqa*) of al-Suhrawardiyya.[82]

His striking denunciation of Ibn 'Arabī is in a particular context, which justifies it, and it is no more than a passing remark. It does not stem from a thorough study, or perhaps indeed, from any study at all of Ibn 'Arabī's thought and works. It is not the whole truth, and cannot be relied upon as a considered judgement.

It seems that 'Izz al-Dīn thought better of Ibn 'Arabī as a spiritual personality, and admired him, but did not agree with, and even criticised, his opinions and sayings which apparently contradicted the canonic teachings of the Sharī'a. In this conclusion I agree with the view of the early mystic, 'Abd al-Ghaffār, quoted above. My point is that a good relationship existed between the two of them. This was demonstrated and discussed at the beginning of this topic. I quote here a unique and interesting story which also sheds light on this good relationship.

As an introduction to a few verses of his own, Ibn 'Arabī says that he once, in a dream, saw 'Izz al-Dīn giving a lecture at which he too was present. After the lecture they sat together. Ibn 'Arabī recited to him some of his verses, extemporised there and then, on the subject of the mercy of God, about which they were conversing. Then one of Ibn 'Arabī's admirers passed by and greeted him cordially, asking his blessing. Ibn 'Arabī kissed him on the lips. 'Izz al-Dīn, observing it, objected to such kissing, saying: 'What is that?' To which Ibn 'Arabī gave a polite and acceptable excuse. The session, in the dream, grew friendlier. 'Izz al-Dīn asked him indirectly of his family affairs. Ibn 'Arabī was inspired and replied in these extaemporary verses:

اذا رأى أهل بيتى الكيس ممتلئا    تبسمت و ذنت منى تمارحنى
وان رائة    خليا    من در اهحه    تكرهت    وانثنت عنى تقابحنى

(i.e. If my wife saw my pocket full, she would smile and approach playfully. If she saw it empty of money she would frown, turn away from me and reproach me).

'Izz al-Dīn smiled and said: 'All of us are like this man with his wife'. Here the dream ended.[83]

The account, although of a dream, suggests their good friendship.

Finally, Ḥj. Khalīfa informs us of a treatise of 'Izz al-Dīn on the lines of saints.[84] This work is of extreme importance for the subject of Ibn 'Arabī's 'Poleship', and 'Izz al-Dīn's authentic view. He would certainly have referred to Ibn 'Arabī, conceding him or denying him his honour. But Ḥj. Khalīfa observes: 'He disproved in it the existence of those saintly figures'. If this observation is accurate the whole story of 'Izz al-Dīn and Ibn 'Arabī's Poleship is exploded. But inaccuracies in Ḥj. Khalīfa's most comprehensive work are not infrequent, and so if we consider the persistent and repeated assertions of the Ṣūfī writers on the subject, we should perhaps, reserve our final judgement until this lost treatise of 'Izz al-Dīn is discovered.[85]

# NOTES

1. The early theologian and mystic of Baghdad (d. 243 A.H.) 'Izz al-Dīn epitomised his chief wrok, *al-Ri'aya*, which L. Massignon (EI, III; 699) wrongly ascribes to 'Izz al-Dīn al-Maqdisī d. 678 A.H.
2. See this dissertation, Chapter, III.
3. The author of most popular treatise *'Awārif al-Ma'ārif*, an orthodox Ṣūfī and the founder of the Suhrawardi *Ṭariqa*, died in Baghdad in 632/1234.
4. Al-Subkī, V; 83, on the authority of Abd 'l-'Azīz al-Hakkāri, the only early compiler of a monograph on 'Izz al-Dīn's life.
5. Abū Shāma p. 133.
6. Abū Shāma, p. 89.
7. The founder of the Shādhilī mystic order, a devout ascetice, died in 656/1258.
8. Al-Kohen al-Fāsī, *Ṭabaqāt al-Shādhiliyya* p. 54, Dr. Margaret Smith, *An Early Mystic of Baghdad*, p. 267.
9. Al-Sha'rānī, *Ṭabaqāt*, I; 163
10. Al-Yāfi'ī., IV; 142, Ibn 'Aṭā' Allāh, *Laṭā'if al-Mihan* p. I; 74, he gives precise details of the gathering; al-Subkī (V; 83) wrongly describes this meeting as being with Abū 'l-Abbās al-Mursī, al-Shādhilī's successor.
11. Al-Sha'rānī, op. cit., II; 6, al-Suyūtī, *Ḥusn.*, II; 173 Iban 'Aṭā' Allāh op. cit., I; 81, he does not ascribe this saying to al-Shādhilī himself, but says that he was told of it.
12. Ibn 'Aṭā' Allāh, I; 76.
13. *Risālat al Karāmāt*... etc. Rasā'il, V; 14.
14. D.B. Macdonald, EI, article: *Karāma.*
15. For a definition of *Karāma* and *Mu'jiza* (miracle performed by a prophet) See R.A. Nicholson *Mystics of Islam*, Ch., 'Saints and Miracles.,
16. Biographical note on 'Izz al-Dīn, Bodleian Ms. Marsh, 428 (unnumbered). This work is wrongly ascribed to Bahā'al-Dīn Ibn Khallikān in the catalogue.
17. Al-Suyūṭī, *Ḥusn.*, II; 173, Ibn Iyās, *Ṭarikh Miṣr*, I; 112.
18. Al-Subkī, V; 82, Ibn al-Mulaqqin, *Ṭabaqāt*, Fol. 72b, Ms. Bodleian, Hunt. 108.
19. Al-Subkī, V; 84 (To indicate the importance of the event he has related it under a separate heading), Ibn al-Mulaqqin op. cit., Fol. 72a, Ibn Iyās, op. cit., Fol. 151a Br. Mus. 18, 514.
20. Al-Maqrīzī, al-Sulūk, I; 354.
21. See this dissertation, Chapter V
22. Al-Subkī, V; 85.
23. See al-Yāfi'ī, *Nashr al-Mahāsin al-Ghāliya*, p. 84, al-Nabhānī, *Jāmi' Karāmāt*.... I; 71-72.

24. 'Izz al-Dīn, *Shajarāt al-Ma'ārif,* Fol. 5a, Ms. Escorial, 1536.
25. See R.A. Nicholson, op. cit., chapter 'Saints and miracles'.
26. For a definition and a brief exposition of this term see Nicholson op. cit., chapter 'Ecstasy'; D.B. Macdonald, EI, article SAMĀ'.
27. *Dhaiyl Mir'āt al-Zamān,* II; 175
28. Al-Dhahabī, *al-'Ibar,* Fol. 286b, Ms. Bodl. Laud, A., 109 he refers to the same source. And he himself, presumably, was the source of the later authors, al-Ṣafadī, Vol. 19, Fol. 4b, al-Yāfi'ī, IV; 154 al-Isnawī, Fol. 129b, Ibn Ḥajar, op. cit., Fol. 62a.
29. Al-'Āmirī, *Ghirbāl al-Zamān* Fol. 72a, Ms. Br. Mus. Add. 21587.
30. *Qawā'id al-Aḥkām,* II; 183
31. *Qawā'id al-Aḥkām,* II; 183.
32. Qur'ān V; 5.
33. *Qawā'id al-Aḥkām,* II; 183
34. Ibid. II; 186.
35. Al-Shādhilī's successor, al-Mūrsī's disciple, and the well known mystic author. The direct sources for 'Izz al-Dīn were, obviously, accessible to him.
36. Muḥ. b. Muḥ. b. Ibrāhim Muḥyi al-Dīn, jurist ṣūfī and poet, died in 662 A.H., in Cairo (Kaḥḥāla, *Mu'jam,* XI; 176).
37. Ibn 'Aṭā'Allāh, op. cit., I; 76-77.

    The last phrase وقام الجميع لقيامه و طاب منه is ambiguous. The text is after the mystical style, as the words used are قوال and قال not المغنى and غنى ('singer' and 'sang'). However, they generally mean the same. Thus, this phrase might suggest a sort of ecstatic excitement, which was later interpreted explicitly as 'dancing'.
38. See D.B. Macdonald's short article: *samā'* in EI.
39. *Qawā'id al-Aḥkām,* II, 179
40. See page 149
41. A.L. Ḥamza, op. cit., p. 204.
42. *Qawā'id al-Aḥkām,* I; 7-8
43. See chapter 5.
44. *Ṭabaqāt,* V; 82.
45. See pages 64-65.
46. A student of 'Izz al-Dīn from Damascus, known as al-Firkāḥ, died in 690 A.H. (al-Subki, V; 60). He used to fetch the books for his master, as he tells us himself.
47. The well known published work on *fiqh.* Ibn 'Arabī was a follower of the Ẓāhirite school of law and presumably brought this work with him from Spain. He also started to epitomise *al-Muhallā* (see al-Qārī al-Baghdādī, *Manāqib* p. 47)
48. Ibn Rajab, *Ṭabaqāt,* II; 140.
49. He was a ṣūfī author and wrote only one work; ***al-Wahīd fī sulūk al-Tauhīd.*** Died in 708 A.H. See Brock. I; 117, S, II; 145.

50. Al-Suyūṭī, *Tabri'at Ibn 'Arabī.* Fol. 3a, MS. Ẓāhiriyya, 5258.

51. This is the general view, thogh disputable as noted by Ibn Ḥajar (*Lisān al-Mīzān* V; 312) and argued against, inadequately, by al-Munāwī.

52. This is remarked by Dr. al-Munajjid. See his recently edited '*manāqib Ibn 'Arabī,* by al-Qārī al-Baghdādī, p. 7. No evidence for the theory is provided. It is actually a repetition of what some early ṣūfī writers such as al-Suyūṭī, al-Munāwī etc. maintain.

53. For the details of these groups see *Manāqib* loc. cit., pp. 25-43 and the introduction to that work by al-Munajjid; Ibn Taymiya, *Madhhab* al-Ittihāḍiyyīn, pp. 75-77; al-Maqqarī, *Nafh*... I; 567-583, al-Sha'rānī, al-Yawāqīt, I; 6-14, Ibn 'l-'Imād, Shadharāt... 192-193.

54. Ibn Taymiya loc. cit. p. 75 (in the Rasā'il collection vol. 4), al-Dhahabī, *Siyar al-Nubala,* Vol. 13, Fol. 231, MS. Aḥmad III, also *al-Wāfī* of al-Ṣafadī, IV; 174.

55. Later a distinguished judge and scholar of repute. It is noteworthy that he was a pious person, conciliatory and cautious in words he spoke; he is not noted as being anti-Ibn 'Arabī. See Ibn Ḥajar, *Lisān al-Mīzān* Vol. 5, and al-Subkī, vol. 6 for his biography. There are a few other transmitters between him and the three sources.

56. The well known author of the biography of the holy Prophet: '*Uyūn al-Āthār*....

57. Ibn Taimiya, op. cit. p. 75.

58. Al-Safadī, IV; 174. Ibn Ḥajar, *Lisān.*, V; 311. In his version of the story there is slight elaboration, and the subject of the unnatural marriage was discussed between them; he had three children from her; after the quarrel she vanished and he never saw her again. Ibn Ḥajar, in his comment dose not consider it a deliberate lie, but a hallucination of Ibn 'Arabī caused by his long recessions and fasting.

59. Thus, with the article, in Spain and in many early Eastern writings.

60. See previous footnote. In EI (II; 361) it is wrongly said to be the *Shuhra* of Ibn 'Arabī in Spain; a mistake copied seemingly from al-Maqqarī, I; 599.

61. A famous old gate in Damascus.

62. Al-Ṣafadī IV; 174

63. Al-Suyūṭī *Tabriāt Ibn 'Arabī,* Fol. 3a.

64. See Ibn 'l-'Imād, V; 193.

65. Jamāl al-Dīn Abū Bakr; he is accused of having introduced many unorthodox opinions into Ibn 'Arabī's works. See al-Sha'rānī, al-Yawāqīt, I; 9.

66. Al-Maqqarī, II; 575, al-Qārī al-Baghdādī op. cit., p. 27-29. This author was a student of al-Fīrūzābādī and relates the story directly from him. Also al-Sha'rānī, *al-Yawāqīt*, I, 13, but his source is Sirāj al-Dīn al-Makhzūmī's (d. 885 A.H.) work,
كشف الغطاء عن اسرار كلام الشيخ محى الدين

67. *Al-Yawāqīt,* I; 11

68. Ibid. I; 12.

69. *Tabri'at Ibn 'Arabī,* Fol. 3b.
70. See footnote 49
71. *Tabri'a,* Fol. lb.
72. *Tabri'a.* Fol. 3b.
73. Ibid., Fol. 1a.
74. Ibid.
75. Ibid.
76. *Al-Ṭabaqāt al-Kubrā,* I; 163 (ed. Cairo, 1925)
77. Ibn 'l-'Imād, *Shadharāt,* V; 193.
78. See Chapter, IV
79. Ibid.
80. Ibn Taymiya, *Madhhab al-Ittihādiyyīn,* p. 76 (Collection of al-Rasā'il, vol. 4).
81. Al-Ṭabaqāt, I; 163, (biographical note on Ibn 'Arabī).
82. The meeting of Ibn 'Arabī and al-Suhrawardī and their mutual complimentary remarks are often quoted in biographical works. The former said of the latter that he was an extreme follower of the Sunna, and we should remember that 'Izz al-Dīn was a disciple of the latter.
83. Ibn 'Arabī's *Diwān* p. 133 (Bombay edition) The whole account is in the lst. person. See also al-Maqqarī, *Nafh.*, II; 571. In it 'Izz al-Dīn's name is replaced by 'Some jurist'.
84. See Chapters II & III.
85. I have tried hard to discover it by searching in the catalogues of Mss. and by corresponding with Istanbul, but no trace of it can be found.

— — —

## CHAPTER—V

# RELIGIO - POLITICAL ACTIVITES

### A SOCIAL AND RELIGIOUS REFORMER

'Izz al-Dīn's reformative activities in the fields of religion and politics are of great significance. His general reputation hangs upon this particular aspect of his life.

He did not devote himself to narrow selfish piety, nor was he a retiring and detached scholar and author. From his earliest days he showed a great interest in the political problems of his times as well as in the religious life of his country.

In the following pages I shall first give a sketch of his religious reformative activities, and then describe the outstanding political events of his life.

In Islam religious, social and political affairs, as is well known, intermingle, and, in fact, there is no such division. Life in all its diverse aspects is one unit, and is governed by a living religion. Ḫowever, for the modern mind it is preferable to introduce some such distinction. The Islamic text: *'al-Amr bi 'l-Ma'rūf wa 'l-Nahy' an 'l-Munkar* includes all sorts of reformative activities, that is, the prescription and promotion of what is good and beneficial, and the proscription and avoidance of what is evil and harmful. But for the sake of clarity we shall here restrict the application of this text to religious and social reformation.

'Izz al-Dīn is noted for his active contribution in this particular field. None of his early or later biographers fail to mention his significance in this. Al-Ṣafadī remarks: كان اماراً بالمعروف نهاءاً عن المنكر لا يخاف فى الله لومة لائم

(i.e. He was a constant and vigorous preacher of good, a persistent proscriber of evil, never fearing the censure of any censurer in the cause of God.)[1].

He criticised 'Alī al-Ḥarīrī[2] for his disregard and renunciation of the injunctions of Islam.[3]

In purely social and administrative spheres he draws our attention to his advice to the Sulṭān of Damascus, al-Ashraf, to abolish the taxes which his corrupt officials had unjustly imposed upon the public, and to redress all the grievances of the oppressed people. When the king requested further advice, he asked him to check his officials who, by their example, encouraged others to indulge in the unlawful pleasures of drink and debauchary. This advice was taken seriously by the Sulṭān, and carried out accordingly.[4]

On another occasion, he advised Najm al-Dīn, King of Egypt, to take action against a similar state of moral corruption in Egyptian society, and criticised him for his inefficient control of public affairs.[5]

He not only criticised the responsible authorities for their lack of proper control over public affairs, and advised them to keep a watchful eye on the moral condition of their people, but also he personally tried to put things right, whenever he got the opportunity or obtained the necessary authority. This he did in Damascus by removing some places of ill-fame[6], and in Cairo, by demolishing the music rooms built by the 'wazir' of the kingdom.[7]

We can well imagine the impact of the words and actions of 'Izz al Dīn. Sovereigns would take notice of the growing decadence, become aware of their responsibilities, and take action to uproot evil and promulgate good. Unjust and corrupt officials and courtiers would be warned and desist from the unfair and oppressive use of their authority. The educated calss (*'Ulamā'*) would be reminded of their moral obligation to check and advise the public and their rulers. The public wolud be stirred to realise their denied rights and oppressed interests. Thus a religious and social awakening would be brought about.

In the purely religious sphere, 'Izz al-Dīn constantly endeavoured to eliminate the prevailing innovations, and purify religion.[8]

He wrote a tract in denunciation of the prevalent religious innovations, particularly that lf a prayer, called 'Ṣalāt al-Raghā'ib' which was commonly offered by many religious doctors and the common people.[9] He was subsequently opposed by some of those who took this prayer for granted. Ibn al-Ṣalāḥ (d. 643 A.H.), the famous traditionist and Shāfi'ite jurist, wrote against 'Izz al-Dīn, and a severe dispute ensued between them. Men of sound scholarship, and scrupulous religious authorities, however, approved 'Izz al-Dīn's viewpoint.[10] And Ibn al-Ṣalāḥ, realising the truth, gave in.[11]

Prompted by conscience, 'Izz al-Dīn advanced this cause not only by his speeches and writings but also by means of his official authority, whenever he held any. His own assertion: 'Blessed be the person who has control over Muslims' affairs, and directs his efforts towards the uprooting of innovations and the restoring of the practice of the Sunna'[12], reveals his attitude in this respect. Naturally, therefore, when he had the power he implemented this 'blessed which'.

Soon after his appointment as the *Khaṭīb* of the great mosque of Damascus, he banned the above-mentioned prayer, and another similar one used on the 15th of the month of Sha'bān. This latter was also an innovation, and such innovations were always disappproved of by the strict orthodox authorities, because they lead people to invent new practices and to introduce them into purely religious matters. This was condemned by the Prophet.

He was so zealous and observant in this respect that even very minor and generally accepted unorthodox practices did not escape his notice, and he abolished them. The preachers of the great Umayyad mosque had adopted certain practices on the occasion of the Friday sermon, such as donning a black cloak, beating the sword on the pulpit, delivering the sermon in rhyme, and praising the present sovereigns. He immediately put an end to all these trivial and formalistic practices. 'He neither wore the usual black cloak, nor rhymed the sermon but spoke unaffectedly in an easy and impressive manner. He also avoided the praise of the Sulṭān, and prayed for him instead'.[13] In order to return more closely to the 'Sunnah' of the Prophet in matters of worship he also stopped the second call (*Adhān*) for the Friday prayer.[14]

Thus 'Izz al-Dīn became the model of a sincere and zealous religious leader, who objectively examines the right features of religion, and then preaches and enforces them faithfully. He never cared for the unsound and unorthodox practices which had infected the community. There are solid grounds for supposing that by these reformative activities of his he greatly inspired the outstanding reformer, Ibn Taymiya, who was born in the year after 'Izz al-Dīn's death (i.e. 661 A.H.). Ibn Taymiya carried on the task more seriously and profoundly, although in a polemical manner which lacked the spiritual charm and appeal of that of his predecessor.

## CONFLICT WITH THE EXTREME HANBALITES

The affairs with which we are now going to deal might also be presented under the heading of 'Kings and 'Izz al-Dīn', for the important stands he took were mostly against Kings, or at least involved them indirectly. But such a heading savours rather of a historical narration. However, if we keep in mind the idea that 'Izz al-Dīn was concerned principally with kings and princes, we shall be better able to grasp the characteristics of his personality as demonstrated in political matters. In fact, these clashes with the ruling authorities play such a celebrated part in his career that his reputation with the general reader rests chiefly upon them.

The first of these incidents was a theological one, and proved a severe trial for 'Izz al-Dīn, involving as it did a direct clash with the Sulṭān of Damascus.

The affair might be called 'Fitnat al-Ḥanābila', for the trial was brought upon him by the Ḥanbalites.

There is a short anonymous monograph on the affair entitled *Qiṣṣat Ibn 'Abd al-Salām*[15]. It did indeed become the story of the time, for the King of Egypt, taking an interest in the matter, wrote to 'Izz al-Dīn and asked him to inform him of the true nature and the details of the unhappy affair. We are indebted to this King for first hand and detailed information on the matter, for he made 'Izz al-Dīn set down the particulars. He did not, however, care to write it down himself, but entrusted his son Sharaf al-Dīn Muḥammad with the task. The son not only recorded the affair in question, but also preserved, or rather added later, some other particulars of his father's life, all of which he incorporated into a small booklet.[16]

Some other early biographers mention the incident briefly, in these words: 'A quarrel arose between the Ḥanbalites and the Shāfi'ites, because of their controversy over a theological question. 'Izz al-Dīn was against the Ḥanbalites, and an uproar ensued. He wrote to al-Malik al-Ashraf...[17], 'He, when in Damascus, suffered much trouble from the Ḥanbalites'[18].

Relying upon the original sources just mentioned, I shall give a detailed account of this affair.

The opposite figure in the incident was al-Malik al-Ashraf (d. 4 Muḥarram 635 A.H.) of Damascus. No date for the incident is given. However, most probably it happened in the year 634 A.H., as suggested by the manner in which it is recorded.

Al-Ashraf was inclined to Ḥanbalite and the Traditionist ideas. He had associated, from his early days, with a fanatical group of Ḥanbalites who maintained that the letters and sounds of the Qur'ān are divine and eternal. Through them he had come to believe that this was the cononical creed, and also the creed of Imām Ibn Ḥanbal and his distinguished followers. This doctrine was so deeply implanted in al-Ashraf's mind that 'anyone who did not believe it was considered by him an infidel deserving of execution'.

'When he learned of 'Izz al-Dīn's profound scholarship and religious influence he was impressed by his reputation, and often wanted to meet him, but 'Izz al-Dīn never visited him'.

We have seen that 'Izz al-Dīn was an Ash'arite. When the group of Ḥanbalites realised that al-Ashraf was favourably disposed towards 'Izz al-Dīn, they tried to turn him against him by stressing his Ash'arite creed. They stirred up the King against him. Their charge was 'that he denounced the believers in the doctrine of the eternity of 'Letters and Sounds of the Qur'ān' as erroneous innovators; and also that he believed in what is maintained by al-Ash'arī, namely that broad does not satisfy, water does not quench thirst, and fire does not burn'. The King considered the allegations too grave to believe, and he accused the Ḥanbalites of being biased against 'Izz al-Dīn. In order to prove their case 'they drafted a number of questions on these theological points, and sent the questionnaire to 'Izz al-Dīn, asking him to reply. They had hoped that 'Izz al-Dīn would reveal his creed in his answers, and would consequently be condemned by the Sulṭān'.

'Izz al-Dīn had heard of their intrigue, and when the paper came to him he emphatically asserted: 'This questionnaire has been composed in order to examine me. I swear, I will write nothing but the truth'.

Then and there he wrote the spirited, explicit and long reply, openly declaring his creed. In it he vigorously supported the Ash'arite doctrine, held by the vast majority of Muslims, and rigorously refuted the points of his adversaries.[19]

His opponents were greatly pleased with this reply, which they could use to incite the Sulṭān against him. They took it to the Sulṭān, he read it, and was infuriated. He exclaimed: 'Indeed, what they accused him of is true. We thought that this man was unique in learning and good in faith. But now it appears that he is irreligious, or rather an unbeliever.

'The Sulṭān uttered these words before a large gathering of religious doctors from different countries at a royal dinner in the month of Ramaḍān. No one dared say anything in defence of 'Izz al-Dīn, but a prominent person among them asked the Sulṭān's pardon for him, particularly in such a month of forgiveness as Ramaḍān. Some others expressed themselves equivocally, as if the creed of 'Izz al-Dīn's adversaries was the right one, and apparently declared their agreement with the king's condemnatory words'.

Thus almost all the '*Ulamā'* betrayed him. Only one scholar stood in 'Izz al-Dīn's defence. He was Ibn al-Ḥājib (d. 646 A.H.), a Mālikite jurist. The news of al-Ashraf's condemnation of 'Izz al-Dīn had spread through the city. Ibn al-Ḥājib went to all the religious authorities who had attended the Sulṭān's meeting. He strongly criticised them for betraying 'Izz al-Dīn even though they held the same doctrine. He even reproached the others who had asked pardon for 'Izz al-Dīn, because the fact that they had done so suggested that he was in the wrong. He pleaded 'Izz al-Dīn's case and aroused them to agree to sign a paper on his behalf.[20]

After this, 'Izz al-Dīn wrote a letter to the Sulṭān, asking him to call a 'debate on the subject which should be attended by all the religious authorities'. This letter shows his courage in addressing an infuriated Sulṭān. He wrote: 'The scholars who were present at the royal gathering have now expressed, in writig, their agreement with my views. They could not express themselves freely beforf the Sulṭān, for they feared his indignation after seeing his angry mood. I believe that if the truth is put before the Sulṭān he will acknowledge it, and punish those who beguiled him with falsehood. He ought to follow his father, Sulṭān al-'Ādil, who inflicted a severe and deterrent punishment on a group of Ḥanbalite innovators, denouncing them as deviationists and discrediting them'.

This outspoken letter, demanding a disputation, made the situation worse. The Sulṭān was more indignant than ever, an immediately wrote a strong reply in his own hand. He refused 'Izz al-Dīn's demand for a debate and declined to meet him. He further accused him of forming a new school of doctrine and creating dissension among the people. The letter ended with the following threat:

'Many an offence committed by the ignorant brings punishment on the innocent.[21] The Tradition says: 'Dissension is sleeping; may God curse him who arouses it'. So, if anyone tries to arouse it, we shall meet him with what will relieve us from our responsibility towards God, and will support His Book, and the Prophet's Sunna'.[22]

'Izz al-Dīn read this letter and, not wishing to act indiscreetly, and to cause a general uproar, chose to remian silent. He said to the messenger; 'I have read the letter and understood; you may go now in peace'. But the Sulṭān intended the letter as a challenge, and wanted complete subservience from him. The messenger replied: 'The royal command is that I should take back an answer'.

However, the conflict between 'Izz al-Dīn and the Sulṭān was only intensified, for 'Izz al-Dīn was not a man to be overawed and intimidated by a royal warning. He was neither shaken nor subdued by the menace. On the contrary, he immediately wrote an outspoken reply defying it. This long letter is indeed, surprisingly downright and sharp in tone. He cites the appropriate condemnatory verses from the Qur'ān, and making clear his position towards the Sulṭān as that of a dutiful adviser,[23] he reasserts his Ash'arite creed. With regard to the accusations that he was mischieviously stirring up dissension among the people and that he intended to establish a fifth 'School of Law', he replied: 'My request for a debate was made from the sense that it was my duty to refute and eradicate false doctrine; religious authorities are bound by God to do that, and it is not the action of a troublemaker. There are no 'schools' for the fundamentals of religion, for they are unanimously agreed upon. Controversies exist only in secondary matters and in details'. He ended the letter with this bold assertion: 'And that we claim that we are of God's party, defenders of His religion, and his soldiers. No soldier who will not risk his life is a true soldier'.[24]

The author who records the affair and who was actually a witness describes the writing of this letter in these words:

'He wrote it fluently, without any pause or hesitation. When he had finished, he sealed it and handed it to the messenger. A respected scholar who used to attend the Sulṭān's court was present at the time. He (i.e. 'Izz al-Dīn) showed him the Sulṭān's letter. The man's face changed colour as he read it and he thought that the Shaykh would not be able to reply to it, because of the Sulṭān's menacing tone. But when he wrote the reply so quickly, before his eyes, the man was astonished, and, in amazement, he remarked: 'If scuh a letter had been received by Quss ibn Sā'ida he would have been bewildered and would not have answered it. But divine providence is with you.[25]

The situation was so hazardous that a man familiar with the temper of the Sulṭān was moved of fear. 'Izz al-Dīn, however, did not panic. He realised what would follow the Sulṭān's threat, but, in spite of that, he fearlessly declared what he believed to be right, caring nothing for the royal anger and the certainty of persecution.

Persecution did, in fact, follow. When the reply was read to the Sulṭān, he was so overcome by fury that the opponents of 'Izz al-Dīn thought that he would undoubtedly be executed'. However, the Sulṭān ordered his wazir, al-Gharz Khalīl, to convey to 'Izz al-Dīn the decree of his punishment, which was: (1) He should deliver no more *fatwās*. (2) He was not to meet anyone. (3) He was to be confined to his house. 'The wazir conveyed to him this decree of forced confinement with great courtesy and regard, for he loved the Shaykh and believed in him.' He also expressed his regret that 'Izz al-Dīn had avoided the Sulāṭn's court, since the Sulṭān had originally greatly desired to meet him.

This unpleasant verdict was, however, no surprise to 'Izz al-Dīn. He received it in good spirits, and said to the sorrowful wazir: 'O'-Gharz, these restrictions are a great benefaction from God, for which I must thank Him.

'As for the issuing of *fatwās*, God knows, I was displeased with the task and disliked it, for I believe that the *muftī* is on the verge of Hell.[26] Had not I believed that God had charged me with the task in these days, I would not have entangled myself with it. Now I have been relieved. The duty has dropped from me, and my responsibility is over. My thanks and gratitude to God.

'As for being forbidden to meet people and being detained in my house, I am not at present at home, but in a summer-house. To stay at home and be completely free for the worship of my Lord is a blessing for me. Fortunate is he who stays in his dwelling and weeps for his sins, and occupies himself with devotion to God. This is a decree of freedom and a favour from God, which He has bestowed upon me through the Sulṭān. He is angry, while I am pleased.

'O' Gharz, God knows that if I had a robe wrothy of the good news which you have brought me I would bestow it on you. However, we are subject to God's providence. Take this prayer-mat; you may perform your prayers on it'. The wazīr accepted the present and respectfully kissed it.

'The wazīr returned to the Sulṭān and informed him of what 'Izz al-Dīn had said to him. Frustrated by this news, the Sulṭān said to his courtiers: "Now, tell me what I can do with this man who receives punishment as a favour."[27]

'Izz al-Dīn remained in solitary confinement, outside the city, for some time. Shortly afterwards an influential religious authority, Jamāl al-Dīn al-Ḥaṣīrī (d. 636 A.H.) the grand Muftī of the Ḥanafites, intervened in the matter. Our original source, describing his visit to the Sulṭān, meticulously records the minutest details, which are of interest, in that they show the dignity and respect he enjoyed in the Sulṭān's eyes. He strongly stressed 'Izz al-Dīn's meritorious qualities and praised him highly in a speech which has already been cited.[28] Al-Ashraf fetched 'Izz al-Dīn's declaration and letter and read them to the Shaykh to demonstrate his case. The Shaykh agreed with 'Izz al-Dīn's views and said: 'Of course, this is the believe of all Muslims and the acknowledged view of righteous people. All that is said in these papers is correct, and if anyone disagrees with it and upholds the other side's theory of the divine qualities of the letters and sounds of the Qur'ān, he is a fool.'

The Sulṭān was duly impressed by this wholehearted defence and this revelation of the correct view. He regretted his decree and ordered 'Izz al-Dīn's release. Moreover, he sent for 'Izz al-Dīn, asked his pardon for what had passed, and sought his company'.[29]

However, 'Izz al-Dīn stayed away from the court, because of his ascetic nature. His victory was yet to be completed.

The 'uproar' to which al-Dhahabī alludes briefly is described in detail in our source, as follows:

'The Ḥanbalites had overcome (after the decree against 'Izz al-Dīn) all the non-Ḥanbalite Ash'arites. Whenever they met with, or passed by Ash'arites in some lonely place they would maltreat them abusing, insulting and beating them. But after al-Ḥaṣīrī's intervention, the Sulṭān ordered both parties to keep silent and not to deliver any *fatwā* on theological matters. This was a step taken to prevent such conflicts. So the Ḥanbalites received a set-back, but the ill-will in their hearts remained'.[30]

Thus the persecution of 'Izz al-Dīn ended with his victory and all was peacefully settled. The victory was, however, not a positive one, as he was forbidden to speak on the subject. It was to be completed by the intervention of the King of Egypt, al-Kāmil, al-Ashraf's elder brother. This Sulṭān was a great lover of sincere religious scholars,[31] and was himself a militant Ash'arite, like almost all the Ayyubid Sulṭāns. Hearing the news of the affair, he wrote to 'Izz al-Dīn and asked to meet him. 'Izz al-Dīn, however, excused himself. The King then asked him to tell him of the affair in detail; his son made a record which he sent to Egypt. Al-Kāmil read it and waited for the opportunity to settle the matter finally.

In due course al-Kāmil came to Damascus, and at his meeting with al-Ashraf, the conversation turned to the partly settled dispute. Al-Kāmil asked his brother what steps had he taken to resolve it. Al-Ashraf said: 'I have forbidden both parties to argue about theological matters'. Al-Kāmil reproachfully remarked: 'What kind of statesmanship and justice is it to treat the right and the wrong equally, to forbid the righteous to perform their duty by preaching the truth, to forbid them to declare what is revealed by God? Your proper course would have been to allow 'Ahl al-Sunna' (i.e. the Ash'arites) to advance proofs for their view, so that they might defend the true doctrine and disseminate it, and to hang perhaps some twenty of the blasphemers, so that the others should be given a warning. At the same time you should have enpowered the righteous theologians to guide the Muslims and to explain to them the right path'.

'Izz al-Dīn's victory was thus complete and the opposite faction was silenced. Al-Ashraf whole-heartedly apologised for what he had done to him, saying: 'We made a great mistake over him'. From then on he constantly tried to please him and to follow his religious opinions. A tract by 'Izz al-Dīn on the prayer entitled *Maqāṣid al-Ṣalā* was read to al-Ashraf three times in one day, and whenever some closefriend called on him he asked his court-reader to recite the tract to him. 'Izz al-Dīn's remark on the Sulṭān's extravagant flattery is interesting and realistic. He says; 'If this tract had been read once to any of the pious students or Ṣūfī adepts he would not have read it or listened to it a second time'. The Sulṭān, however, either because he genuinely admired it, or because he wished to compensate its author, offered the tract to a great historian and preacher, Sibṭ Ibn al-Jauzī (d. 654 A.H.), a friend and frequent visitor of the Ayyubid Sulṭāns; the historian read it in his presence and praised it. The Sulṭān asked him to recommend it to the public at his coming speech in the great mosque of Damascus, which he did. In consequence of this countless copies of the tract were copied and circulated.[32]

'Izz al-Dīn, however, was not much impressed by these marks of favour, just as he had not previously been frightened by the Sulṭān's threats, and still stayed away from the court. He called on the Sulṭān, at the latter's request, only when he was ill, in fulfilment of the religious obligation of visiting the sick. He used this one meeting which he had with al-Ashraf to advise him on some social and religious reforms.[33]

We can easily imagine the effect of this first bold stand of 'Izz al-Dīn on the contemporary religious authorities, the majority of whom dared not express themselves freely in the presence of an angry Sulṭān. They later saw how the truth triumphed, and how sincerity and courage were rewarded; an impressive lesson for the hypocritical religious leaders, who were over-fond of compromise. 'Izz al-Dīn's truthfulness and moral courage also impressed the sovereigns of his time, for it was because al-Kamil of Egypt was so impressed by these qualities of his that he was moved to defend him; others, too, like al-Ṣāliḥ Ismā'īl, the successor of al-Ashraf, and Najm al-Dīn of Egypt, took lessons for the future.

## CLASH WITH AL-ṢALIḤ ISMA'IL, THE RULER OF DAMASCUS

'Izz al-Dīn's second remarkable stand was of a purely political nature. It occurred in 638 A.H.

Al-Ṣāliḥ Ismā'īl succeded al-Ashraf as ruler of Damascus in 635 A.H. From the beginning of his rule political enmity existed between him and his nephew, Najm al-Dīn of Egypt. Najm al-Dīn had suffered much personal injury from Ismā'īl when, after a desperate struggle he had settled himself on the throne of Egypt, he wished to take revenge upon his uncle.

Al-Ṣāliḥ Ismā'īl, fearing the advance of his nephew against Damascus, swiftly made an alliance with the Crusaders, who were occupying some of the coastal towns of Syria. By the terms of this treaty he ceded to them the territories of Safad and Ṣhaqīf, along with their two strong forts, the remaining half of Type, Tiberias, 'Āmila hillside and all the coastal provinces.[34] Most of these places were of great strategic importance, and were coveted strongholds.

Furthermore, he allowed the Franks to enter Damascus, and to buy arms there. The inhabitants of Damascus were concerned at this development, and some conscientious arms dealers referred the matter to 'Izz al-Dīn's judgement. He strongly opposed the sale of arms to the Crusaders, and issued a *fatwā* to that effect.[35]

He further criticised the Sulṭān, Ismā'īl, from the pulpit of the great Mosque of Damascus at a Friday sermon. He had been accustomed to pray for the Sulṭān of the time in his sermons, but now he dropped the mention of Ismā'īl's name, and even prayed against him, asking God's help in putting matters to rights.[36] That is to say, 'he started to incite the people against the Sulṭān', as a historian explicitly says.[37]

Al-Ṣāliḥ Ismā'īl was away from Damascus. When the news of this open criticism reached him he immediately dispatched an order for 'Izz al-Dīn's dismissal from the post of the *Khiṭāba,* and for his arrest. Ibn al-Ḥājib was also arrested, for siding with 'Izz al-Dīn. Both of them were imprisoned in the fort of Damascus.[38]

When the Sulṭān returned to the capital he ordered their release, after being subjected to some pressure and many requests.[39]

However, it was not a complete release for 'Izz al-Dīn, for he was confined to his house with orders not to meet anyone and not to issue any *fatwās*. He was only permitted, at his request, to go out for the Friday prayer, an to receive the physician and barber when necessary.[40]

But this dull solitary life during such a period of political crisis became intolerable for him, and he decided to leave the country. Having received permission, he set out for Egypt in 638 A.H. and arrived in Cairo in 639 A.H.[41] This indicates that the clash in question took place about the end of 638 A.H.

On his way to Cairo, he stopped at Jerusalem. In this city he was again disturbed by al-Ṣāliḥ Ismā'īl, who had arrived there with his allies to meet the hostile Egyptians. Ismā'īl wanted to win 'Izz al-Dīn back and sent a messenger to him with orders to persuade him to returne to Damascus, where he would be given his previous office and several new ones besides. 'Otherwise', the Sulṭān ordered the messenger, 'arrest and detain him in the tent next to mine.[42]

The messenger conveyed this promise to 'Izz al-Dīn making the sole condition that, to show his obedience, he should kiss the Sulṭān's hand. To this conditional offer 'Izz al-Dīn gave a reply which will be long remembered in history as that of an undaunted, resolute and stoical man. He said to the messenger: 'My poor fellow, I swear that I should not even like him to kiss my hand. Oh men! you are in one world, and I am in another world. Thanks to God who has plagued you with that from which He has protected me'. Eventually he was arrested and detained in a tent, as had been ordered.[43]

An interesting event followed his arrest. 'Izz al-Dīn was chanting the Qur'ān one day, and was heard by the Sulṭān and some of his allied Frankish knights. The next day the Sulṭān said to the knight: 'Did you hear that man chanting the Qur'ān?' 'Yes', they said. 'He is', said the Sulṭān, 'the grand pastor of the Muslims (اكبر قوس المسلمين). I imprisoned him, and dismissed him from his offices, for criticising my ceding the Muslim forts to you. Afterwards I expelled him from the country. Now I have rearrested him for your sake'. The knights, in reply to this flattering speech, said: 'Were he our pastor we would have washed his feet and drunk the water'.[44]

A later reliable source, Ibn Ḥājar (d. 851 A.H.) says that he was then released through the mediation of the kinghts.[45]

The original source, 'Izz al-Dīn's son, on the other hand, informs us that he was released after the Egyptian forces arrived and won the battle of Jerusalem. This statement seems to me more probable than the former.

'Izz al-Dīn then proceeded to Cairo, where he was warmly welcomed by Sulṭān Najm al-Dīn, and was appointed the chief qāḍī of Egypt, as we have seen.

Here he again came into conflict with the absolute Sulṭān and some of the most powerful officials of the Kingdom. I give an account of these events in chronological order, with comments where necessary.

## AUCTIONING OF THE MAMLUK VASSAL PRINCES

The first and the most outstanding event of 'Izz al-Dīn's life in Egypt was the case which is remembered as 'The sale by action of some slave Turkish princes'. This is, indeed, a most amusing and courageous case in legal history, and is related, originally, by al-Subkī. It has been much popularised by later writers and has gained 'Izz al-Dīn a unique reputation.[46]

Before giving an account of this case it seems necessary to say something of the origin of these vassal princes.

Al-Ṣāliḥ Najm al-Dīn, who was his father's viceroy in the Mesopotamian territories of the Ayyubid Empire, had gathered together a large number of Turks, enslaved in wars or bought, for his army. They were collectively known as Turks, but were, in fact, of mixed origins: Turkumans, Armenians, Byzantines (al-Rūm), Circassians etc. Turks, however, formed the majority and were most prominent.[47]

When Najm al-Dīn came back to Egypt to occupy his father's seat in Cairo this slave army came with him and helped him to secure the throne. These Mamlūks thus became his chief military power. They were the same who later formed the strong ruling dynasty of the Mamlūks. Some of their chiefs were even given the title of prince by the Sulṭān.

When 'Izz al-Dīn took office as chief qāḍī, these Mamlūk princes were at the zenith of their power.[48]

'He found that these princes had not been legally freed, and thus, from the legal standpoint were still slaves. He issued a decree announcing their slave status, which implied that they could not act as free citizens, according to the law of the time. He did, in fact, refuse to ratify any contracts that they made, financial or civil, that is to say, concerning the sale and purchase of property: marriage and divorce, etc.' This was a great annoyance to them and made their lives very difficult.

Among these Mamlūks was the Viceroy of the Kingdom (نائب السلطنة), who was infuriated by this humiliation. The princes met together and sent for 'Izz al-Dīn. They asked him what he wanted to do with them. He said: 'I shall call a court meeting an there you shall be put up for sale for the public treasury (بيت مال المسلمين), and will thus be legally freed'.[49]

Seeing that the chief qāḍī was determined on this 'they took the matter to the Sulṭān (Najm al-Dīn). The Sulṭān asked 'Izz al-Dīn to spare them and to drop the case, but he refused. The indignant Sulṭān severely rebuked 'Izz al-Dīn, and accused him of interfering in a matter which was not his concern'.

'Izz al-Dīn was angry, and in protest against the Sulṭān's interference in a case of law, resigned and resolved to quit the country. As the original source says: 'He actually loaded his luggage on one ass, mounted his family on another, and set out, himself on foot, from Cairo for Syria'. He had not gone half a league, when a large number of people, men, women, children, an in particular, religious doctros, pious people and merchants, caught up with him and joined him.

'The news of this (mass exodus) reached the Sulṭān, and he was warned that if the Shaykh went away his Kingdom would be gone. He immediately rode out himself, caught 'Izz al-Dīn up, asked his pardon and appeased him. 'Izz al-Dīn then returned to Cairo, on condition that the decree in question should be put into effect'.

The Viceroy now approached him directly, politely requesting him to drop the case; but this also did not work. The Viceroy lost his temper and, in a fury, arrogantly cried: 'How can this Shaykh auction us while we are the lords of the land? I swear that I will strike off his head with this sword of mine'.

Furious and determined to kill 'Izz al-Dīn, 'he came with a few of his men to his house, holding an unsheathed sword in his hand. At his knock 'Izz al-Dīn's son came out, and frightened by what he saw, went in and informed his father. 'Izz al-Dīn, unshaken and undisturbed, pacified his son, saying humbly: "O my son, your father is not worthy to be killed in the path of God" (i.e. for the sake of establishing His law). He then came out fearlessly, as if he were divine fate descending upon the Viceroy. The moment he glanced at the Viceroy his hand was stiffened, the sword fell from it and he began to tremble. Shedding tears, he begged 'Izz al-Dīn to pray for him'. Then, turning to the vital matter, he asked him: 'O Sir, tell me what you intend to do' 'Auction you' replied 'Izz al-Dīn. 'What would the price money be spent on?' asked the other. 'On public welfare' came the reply. 'Who would collect it?' the viceroy asked. 'I', answered 'Izz al-Dīn.

His decision was carried out. He auctioned the princes one by one, and demanded high prices; he collected the money and spent it on public welfare.'

After this detailed account, al-Subkī remarks: 'Such a thing is related of no one else.'[50]

I have told the story of the affair in the words of the original authority, and I shall now attempt to discuss it.

It is a singular case. Some later authorities, historians and biographers, also mention it briefly[51] but their source is, almost certainly, al-Subkī. It is surprising that 'Izz al-Dīn's son, who recorded some of the outstanding religious and political events of his father's life in the monograph already mentioned does not mention the case at all. In fact, he gives only a brief account of his father's life in Egypt, for there are some other events, recorded elsewhere, which he does not mention. Nevertheless, while enumerating 'Izz al-Dīn's posts in Egypt,[52] he makes what may be an allusion to this affair: 'While he occupied these posts, he performed some very singular deeds.[53] He also mentions 'Izz al-Dīn's resigning twice. The cause of his second resignation is mentioned in many other sources, and thus the occasion of his 'first resignation, after which he returned to his post as qāḍī',[54] was certainly this case of the Mamlūk princes. This, then, is the earliest piece of evidence from a direct source, (al-Subkī, although earlier, and the chief source for 'Izz al-Dīn, is not a direct source). The reliable annalists of the Ayyūbid period never allude to this strange event.

Modern essayists such as al-Rāfi'ī and Ṭanṭāwī,[55] and scholars such as al-Maghribī,[56] Dr. A. Ḥamza,[57] Maḥmūd, R. Saleem,[58] take the case for granted and cite it as an example of 'Izz al-Dīn's moral courage and sense of duty. Their source is also al-Subkī.

Recently (1959), the famous Egyptian playwright, Taufīq al-Ḥakīm, wrote a play السلطان الحائر based on this case.[59]

The producer of the play actually mentions this case of 'Izz al-Dīn's as that which forms the plays' historical basis.[60]

It has been studied and historically and analytically criticised by the noted scholar and critic, Amīn al-Khūlī, in an Egyptian periodical.[61]

The playwright, in his preface, describes the main point of the play as: 'A conflict between the Sulṭān and the Qāḍī; between the executive and the judicial authorities; between the sword and the law.'

This is accurate and in accordance with the historical facts but Taufīq al-Ḥakīm has greatly confused, or even distorted, the characters. In the play the Sulṭān himself is a slave whom the Qāḍī is determined to auction, and the wazir is a free man. The worst mistake is that the Qāḍī (i.e. 'Izz al-Dīn) is represented as being reluctant, hypocritical and unsuccessful. This is the fault of the playwright's personal views and prejudices.

I felt it necessary to make this brief observation on the play, in order to show that, although the author claimed that his main characters were historical personages, the plot is, in fact, historically quite inaccurate.

The point which I wish to make is that the learned critic of the play also took the case in question for granted, again copying from al-Subkī, in his attempt to reveal the historical background of the play.[62]

So much for the authenticity of this odd case.

The astonishing fact is that in spite of its being an outstanding, and indeed unique event in legal history, none of the Mamlūk princes in the case is identified in any of the sources. It is even more surprising, when we reflect that a Viceroy of the Kingdom was included in the auction.

It is astonishing, however, that not ony the essayists but scholars also, although they express great admiration for 'Izz al-Dīn's courage in this case, have failed to remark what is, to me, one of its most singular points; the fact that none of the princes, not even the Viceroy, has been identified.

It is, perhaps, this lack of identification which makes a later writer Ibn al-Mulaqqin (d. 809 A.H.) qualify his account of the case with the vague phrase: 'it is said (و حكى).[63] It is presumably the strangeness of the case and the lack of identification which makes Brockelmann, too, (suppl. I; 768) allude to it briefly: 'he (Izz al-Dīn) legally disqualified some Turkish princes in Cairo'.

Only Maḥmūd R. Saleem felt the case to be a peculiar one. He, however, ended by accepting it although he produced no evidence other than the fact that al-Subkī's detailed and circumstantial account leaves not doubt as to its actual occurence. He did not raise the question of the identity of the princes and the principal figure, the Viceroy.

In fact, in spite of brief notices such as these, this extermely strange case has never been objectively studied. I was first made sceptical, and consequently had to discuss the case in detail, by the fact that the Viceroy is not identified. Since this is an objection which will, I suppose, occur to every reader, I fetl that I should make every effort to discover the identity at least of this one important figure.

Seeing that 'Izz al-Dīn held the post of the chief qāḍī for one year only, (640 A.H.), during the reign of Najm al-Dīn and the Viceroy was one of very few most powerful officials of the kingdom, the task of identification and of reaching a satisfactory conclusion seemed possible to me.

The Arab annalists carefully record all the important and even many of the trivial events of each year, but of this extraordinary event (we should recall the public protest and the Sulṭān's concern and immediate action) there is no trace in any of the contemporary or reliable later annals of the year.

Najm al-Dīn appointed several of his Mamlūk military chiefs or vassal princes as Viceroys, at different perids, to represent him in Damascus or in Cairo, when he himself was absent. They were, indeed, specifically called نائب السلطنة. Among them were Rukn al-Dīn Baybars, (later Sulṭān al-Ẓāhir..), Jamāl al-Dīn Yaghmūr and Ḥusām al-Dīn al-Hadhabānī, to mention only the most celebrated. None of these, however, or indeed, anyone else, represented the Sulṭān in Cairo in the year when 'Izz al-Dīn was the chief qāḍī. I perused the accounts of their lives in contemporary and other early histories to see if I could find any hint of the affair, but in vain.

It might be supposed that the last of the men I mentioned (i.e. al-Hadhabānī) entitled al-Amīr (prince), was the Viceroy who figured in the case. The evidence to support this view derives from another case concerning this prince and 'Izz al-Dīn, in the time of the latter's qadiship, when he refused to accept the prince as a witness for the Sulṭān.[64] This case is very well attested, for it is recorded by the prince himslef. No reason is given, however, for 'Izz al-Dīn's refuṣal to accept him as a witness. It was perhaps that, in 'Izz al-Dīn's view, al-Hadhbānī had only slave status.[63]

I cannot be sure that al-Hadhbānī was among the Turkish slave chiefs. However, his grandfather's name, Bashak, (which might be written with P in its non-Arabic form) indicates that he was not of Arab origin, and might be of Kurdish, Armenian or Turkish origin, and that he might have been one of those who came with Najm al-Dīn from those regions.

The riddle of the Viceroy is partially solved by al-Subkī himself, later. In his shorter unpublished version of *al-Ṭabaqāt,* where he again recorded the affair, he crossed out the words (نائب السلطنة) (the Viceroy) which he corrected in the margin to اتابک العسكر (commander - in-chief) and most high prince of the time'.[66]

The chief prince of the story, then, was not a Viceroy, as has been popularly supposed, owing to al-Subkī's earlier inaccurate statement, but was the military chief. Al-Hadhabānī was, in fact, the most powerful chief and the one who was most loyal, and most dear, to Najm al-Dīn. He had served his master in his earlier destitute state, before he became Sulṭān of Egypt, when all the other Mamlūk chiefs of his army had left him in Palestine.[67]

The legal point in ʻIzz al-Dīn's acting thus sternly with these vassal princes only, and not all the other thousands of Mamlūks in Najm al-Dīn's army, was that these princes held the important administrative and military posts which a person of slave status is not allowed to hold. ʻIzz al-Dīn, therefore, determined to put right a state of affairs which was legally inadmissible, and which was also of considerable importance.

As well as ʻIzz al-Dīn's exemplary sense of duty as a judge, we may also admire his noble desire to benefit the poor with the money obtained by the sale of these feudal lords.

A modern writer, also a judge, has tactfully rescued these princes from the disgrace of having been sold, by stating that the Sulṭān himself paid the money demanded for them.[68]

To sum up, even if the identity of these princes is not established and the supposed identity of the main character is doubtful, or even proved to be false, the main features of the case are beyond doubt. It is unjust and unscientific to imagine that the whole story was fabricated by al-Subkī. As far as his own direct source is concerned, it is likely that he drew on some work which is unknown to us.[69] The reakness of his account, his failure to mention the names of the Mamlūk princes, is due, probably, to the fact that these same Mamlūks shortly afterwards became the masters and rulers of both Egypt and Syria. In al-Subkī's time their descendants were still the rulers of the Empire, and it would obviously be dangerous for him to mention the names of the Mamlūk Sulṭān's, governers' or military chiefs' fathers or kin in connection with anything so disgraceful as a slave auction. The same argument applies to the contemporary or later popular historians, who were in most cases closely attached to, and patronised by, the Mamlūk Sulṭāns and princes.

To conclude, I am inclined to believe that the case occurred, in spite of the unhistorical nature of al-Subkī's account, which I have tried, as far as possible, to fit in with the historical facts.

ʻIzz al-Dīn's general character, and his reputed strictness and courage strengthen my belief.

## A DECREE AGAINST THE EGYPTIAN WAZIR

The next courageous stand that ʻIzz al-Dīn took was against a wazir of the Egyptian Kingdom, in the same year, is 640 A.H., and is historically much more vividly and fully documented.

The wazir in this case was Mu'īn al-Dīn Ḥasan b. Shaykh al-Shuyūkh[70] (d. 643 A.H.) He was the most powerful of the four sons of Shaykh al-Shuyūkh Ibn Ḥamawayh al-Juwaynī, three of whom held the highest posts, as wazīrs and generals, in the Ayyūbid kingdom of Egypt.[71]

The power and honour which Mu'īn al-Dīn enjoyed is demonstrated by a quotation from a scrupulous historian, al-Maqrīzī: 'The Sulṭān treated him with royal honours, as his equal. He was allowed to sit at the head of the royal dinner table, and to go riding in the kingly manner. The Sulṭān also ordered that his chamberlain, Shihāb al-Dīn Rashīd, should stand to serve the wazīr at table, and that the chief of the cavalry and the chamberstaff should stand in his presence, as if he were the Sulṭān himself.[72]

It was this wazir who had a music hall built on the roof oa a mosque in Cairo. 'Izz al-Dīn, as a chief qāḍī of the Kingdom condemned this act of sacrilege. Taking immediate action against the profane behaviour of the wazīr he went himself with his sons, demolished the building and cleared the roof. He then declared the wazīr disqualified from witnessing in court, and resigned, in protest.[73] Al-Ṣafadī says: 'He knew that the Sulṭān and the wazir would be enraged (by the demolition). 'His resignation' al-Ṣafadī continues 'grieved the Sulṭān'[74] because, perhaps, he knew well the high qualities and the sincerity of his qāḍī. However, he accepted his resignation.

'Izz al-Dīn's decree against the wazīr, that is, the legal withdrawal of confidence, was of considerable consequence. The following case denotes the gravity of the issue and the power of 'Izz al-Dīn's word, even in the exalted court of the Caliphate in Baghdad.

The wazīr thought that he would not be affected by this decree abroad, but it happened that the Sulṭān sent a message to the Claiph al-Musta'ṣim, in Baghdad. The messenger was asked at the Caliph's court: 'Did you receive this message from the Sulṭān?' 'No, but Ibn Shayk al-Shuyūkh, the wazir, gave it to me on behalf of the Sulṭān', the messenger replied. 'He', rejoined the Caliph, 'has been declared untrustworthy, so we cannot accept his word'. The emissary then came back to Cairo,and the Sulṭān personally gave him the message, which he again delivered to Baghdad'.[75]

Relating the affair, 'Abd al-Qādir al-Maghribī, the late vice president of the Arab Academy, Damascus, comments; 'His word was as powerful as the word of the Popes of Rome in the Middle Ages. Al-'Izz ibn 'Abd al-Salām's disqualifying Fakhr al-Dīn[76] b. Shaykh al-Shuyūkh in this way is analogous to the excommunication of Christians by the Church authorities.[77]

The comment is interesting, though the comparison and analogy are not obviously relevant. It does, however, emphasise the effectiveness of 'Izz al-Dīn's word.

## WITH QUTUZ DURING THE TARTAR INVASION

The Tartars, after the destruction of Baghdad, advanced into Syria, conquering and subduing its cities. They were later to march victoriously westward to Egypt.

At this time the young al-Manṣūr Alī, the son of Mu'izz al-Dīn Aybak, the first King of the Mamlūk dynasty, was on the throne of Egypt. A general, Quṭuz, was his regent.

'Izz al-Dīn was now about 80, and was a notable and respected religious authority, engaged in the quiet profession of teaching in a college. His advice was still, however, sought in grave crises, as the following case shows.

Frightened by the devastating advance of the Tartars, the King of Aleppo al-Nāṣir, sought Egyptian help in confronting them and defending his territories. Ibn al-'Adīm (d. 660 A.H.), the renowned historian, came to Cairo in 657 A.H. as Syrian emissary to request this help.[78]

Quṭuz called a meeting of the generals, the qāḍīs and other notables, to seek their advice, and they assembled in the state court of the Hill Fort. 'Izz al-Dīn also attended the assembly, along with the chief qāḍī of the Kingdom Badr al-Dīn al-Sanjarī. The young Sulṭān al-Manṣūr was seated on his throne.

When the assembly was complete, a court spokesman raised the question of Hūlagū's march, the capitultion of all the cities which he passed, and his arrival in Aleppo. He said: that the public treausry was empty, the Sulṭān was a young child and the natinon's peace and welfare were in jeopardy. The most pressing need, therefore, was to choose a responsible monarch, whom people would fear, and who could stand against the enemy. Moreover, the treasury required a subsidy from the public to raise a strong army, and to provide them with what they need to march against the enemy.[79]

Thus the regent, Quṭuz, had schemed to have himself pronounced King, and thus to collect heavy taxes for the army from the common people.

The man who spoke at that critical moment was 'Izz al-Dīn. The historians tell us that what he said represented the will of the whole assembly, although none of the great men there, not even the chief qāḍī, dared to oppose or dispute the proposal of the court spokesman. 'Izz al-Dīn, however, quashed the second part of this proposal.[80] He said:

'If an enemy invades a Muslim country, it is incumbent upon all to fight in defence of it. It is permissible to collect whatever is needed to finance the war, provided that none of the precious gilded and ornamented arms and saddles, the 'embroidered hoods' and the jewelled staffs and swords, etc. are left in the treasury; provided also that you sell your golden girdles and other valuables, and that every soldies has only his arms and riding animal and that he is on a level with al the common people. But it is not permissible to raise money from the people while the eminent soldiers keep their properties and valuable arms.[81]

This was, as the historians we have cited, say the speech which concluded the meeting. The newly proclaimed King Quṭuz accepted 'Izz al-Dīn's advice. It is said that 'Izz al-Dīn also encouraged him, saying: 'If you follow the right course, I guarantee that you will win the battle, by the grace of God'.[82]

Not only did this speech of 'Izz al-Dīn's save the common people from having their money unjustly seized, but it also gave a moral impetus to the King and army chiefs, raised the soldiers' morale, and, at the same time, induced citizens to participate willingly in the defence of their country. Quṭuz with his army, met the Tartars in a decisive battle shortly afterwards at the 'Goliatn Spring' in Palestine, in 658/1259. As 'Izz al-Dīn had predicted, the Muslim army was victorious, and for the first time, the invincible hords were defeated and pursued from the field, and thier further westward advance was halted.

'Izz al-Dīn himself could not take part in the battle, because of his advanced age, but his sound advice and encouragement is well remembered and acknowledged by historians.

## RELATIONS WITH AL-NĀSIR OF PALESTINE AND BAYBARS OF EGYPT

Another Ayyubid monarch with whom he came in contact, and who wished him to stay in his tiny Kingdom, al-Karak (Palestine), was al-Nāṣir Dāwūd[83] (d. 656 A.H.) We have seen, in the first chapter, that this monarch invited 'Izz al-Dīn, after he had been exiled from Damascus, to reside in his Kingdom, and eagerly pressed him to do so. But when 'Izz al-Dīn bluntly refused, and said: 'Your country is too small for my learning', he was disappointed.

The enraged Sulṭān later expressed his anger in a letter to 'Izz al-Dīn, taking advantage of a political disaster. Not long after 'Izz al-Dīn's refusal (in 640 A.H.)[84] Nabulus, a city of this Sulṭān's Kingdom, was sacked in a surprise attack by the Crusaders. The Sulṭān, in his grief, wrote a long letter to Izz al-Dīn addressing him as ( المجلس السامى ), القضوى الفرى and reproached him for not urging the people of Cairo to defend his city. This strongly phrased letter shows, indirectly, the power of 'Izz al-Dīn's word on people, and how it was sought in time of need.

Here is a passage from the letter, 'O, 'Izz al-Dīn we thought that the spell of your determined will would be the amulet against the witchcraft of the infidels. The general call to arms was announced in Syria, and it was the duty of blooming youth and old men alike to fight in defence of their country. O, tongue of the Sharī'a, where was your campaigning skill and courage. If the sharp Indian sword was blunt, where was the keen sword of your tongue! Did you sheathe it when the swords of the infidels were unsheathed[85]?'

The letter continues in the same ornate and vigorous language.

Another reason for al-Nāṣir's bitter feelings was, presumably, the fact that 'Izz al-Dīn accepted the offer of al-Nāṣir's enemy, Najm al-Dīn, and resided in his Kingdom, Egypt.

It seems that there was more correspondence between this Sulṭān and 'Izz al-Dīn. For Abu 'l-Fidā, mentioning the *mukātaba* (correspondence) between them, also records some verses from a poem which the Sulṭān wrote to 'Izz al-Dīn.[86] However, they are a sort of literary lamentation, and do not mention 'Izz al-Dīn at all.

In his later years he saw the rise of the power of the Mamlūk dynasty, when its most powerful and celebrated king, al-Ẓāhir Baybars, settled himself on the Egyptian throne, immediately after defeating the Tartars with Quṭuz. 'Izz al-Dīn was still strong enough to check this triumphant and tyrannical monarch, on legal grounds. It is said that when he attended Baybars,' ceremonial proclamation of the sovereignty, he outspokenly addressed the King: 'O Rukn al-Dīn, I know you as a bondman of al-Bunduqdār'.[87] He would not pledge his allegiance to him until someone rose to witness the transference of his bondage to al-Sālih Najm al-Dīn, and then his being freed.[88]

Baybars later admitted that 'Izz al-Dīn's words had great influence. He watched 'Izz al-Dīn's huge funeral procession pass the castel, and said: 'Today my rule has been settled, for if this Shaykh had incited the people to rebel against me, they would have snatched away my rule from me'.[89]

In 659 A.H. when a caliph named Aḥmad, of the Abbāsid family of Baghdad, was proclaimed the legitimate caliph, with the title of al-Mustanṣir, 'Izz al-Dīn was present at the ceremony. After the two principal official authorities, King Baybars and the chief qāḍī, he was the first to pronounce his acknowledgement of, and allegiance to, the new Caliph.[90]

He dealt with several Sulṭāns, criticising and checking them on some occasions, directing and advising them on others; he was always fearless and acted from the highest motives. In this way, he reminded the sovereigns of their duties of government, and created political awareness in the public. Mentioning these events in 'Izz al-Dīn's life, and his moral courage, a modern writer, Dr. Ḥamza rightly remarks: 'He was most qualified to be the religious and social leader of his time.[91]

# NOTES

1. Al-Wāfī, Vol 19, Fol. 4b. See also al-Subkī, V; 80, al-Kutbī, I; 595, Ibn al-'Imād, V; 302 etc.
2. A popular and influential *darwīsh*, founder of the Ḥarīriyya *darwīsh* order, who die in 645 A.H. in Damascus.
3. Al-Nu'aimī, *al-Dāris*, II; 172. This man and his followers were alleged to be libertines, see Ibn Kathīr, XIII; 173.
4. Al-Subkī, V; 99
5. See Chapter, VI
6. Al-Subkī, V; 99.
7. See Chapter V
8. Al-Yāfi'ī, IV; 153, Ibn al-Mulaqqin, *Ṭabaqāt al-Shāfi'iyya,* Fol. 71, Ms. Bodl. Hunt., 108.
9. Ḥj. Khalīfa, IV; 107
10. Al-Yāfi'ī, IV; 155
11. Al-Subkī, V; 105. He preserves a letter of 'Izz al-Dīn to his opponent as a supplement to the biography of the former, V; 105-107.
12. His letter, just mentioned, in al-Subkī, V; 107
13. Ibn al-'Imād, V; 302
14. Ibn al-Mulaqqin, op. cit., Fol. 71a. Such is still the practice of some orthodox groups in Muslim countries.
15. Ms. Leyden, cod. or. 644 (27)
16. This monograhp is incorporated by al-Subkī in his biography of 'Izz al-Dīn, *Ṭabaqāt* V; 85-102. Al -Subkī wrongly attributes it to 'Abd al-Laṭīf, another son of 'Izz, al-Dīn. It has also been printed separately in Cairo (n.d.) with the title' ايضاح الكلام فى مسئلة او كلام

    I have used a Ms. copy (Princeton, yahuda 1847) of this monograph, in the author's autograph, and also *'Qiṣṣat Ibn 'Abd al-Salām'* of Leyden. But as these both are unnumbered the references are given from al-Subkī.
17. Al-Dhahabī, *Siyar al-Nubalā'*, II; Fol. 294, Ms. Ahmad 11129/0, the next part of the text is mutilated.
18. Al-Ṣafadī, 19; Fol. 5a, al-Kutubī, I; 596
19. See Chapter, II
20. For the text of his speech see al-Subkī, V; 92
21. The verse is: و جرم جره سفهاء قوم محل بغير جانيه العذاب
22. For the full text of the letter see al-Subkī, V; 93
23. According to the famous Prophetic tradition, it is incumbent upon Muslims to advise their ruler.

24. For the full text see al-Subkī, V; 93-95.

25. Al-Subkī, V; 95.

26. B ecause of the delicacy of the task and the responsibility he assumes for his decisions, which may be wrong or unjust.

27. Al-Subkī; V; 95.

28. See Chapter II.

29. Al-Subkī, V; 97.

30. Al-Subkī, V; 97.

31. He gathered a number of distinguished scholars about him, and so keen was his thirst for knowledge, and so intense his desire for the company of the learned, that he had beds placed for some of them beside his own. In this way he was enabled to listen to their talk late into the hight. See al-Maqrīzī;1, 259.

32. Al-Subkī, V; 98.

33. See Chapter V.

34. Al-Maqrīzī, I; 303: the other historians such as Sibṭ Ibn al-Jauzī, Abū Shāma, Abū 'l-Fidā, Ibn Khaldūn etc. mention briefly the first two places, as they were the most important. The Shaqif Fort is the famous Bell Fort of the Latin chronicles (Hitti, *History of Arabs*, p. 606.) A monograph entitled قلعه الشقيف on the history of this fort was written by Sulayman al-Zāhir of Lebanon. (Mj. *al-'Irfan*, Vol. 48, No. 7, p. 624).

35. Al-Yūnīnī, II; 173, al-Maqrīzī, I; 303, al-Subkī, V; 100.

36. Al-Maqrīzī, I; 304, al-Subkī, V; 100.

37. Ms. Camb. Add. 2925, Anon., Annals of the year 638 A.H.

38. Abū Shāma, p. 170.

39. Al-Subkī, V; 101

40. Al-Maqrīzī, I; 304.

41. Abū Shāma, p. 171

42. Al-Subkī, V; 101. This and further details are taken from the account of 'Izz al-Dīn's son, preserved in al-Subkī.

43. Al-Subkī, V; 101

44. Ibid, V; 101

45. Ibn Ḥajar, Fol. 62, in this source there are no such details but he does mention the displeasure of the knights.

46. See al-Rāfi'ī, Wḥyi *al-Qalam*, III; 58-66, essay: امراءللبيع 'Alī Ṭantāwī, *Rijāl min al-Tārīkh*, pp. 223-233 essay: شيخ من دمشق

47. Ibn Khaldūn, *Tārīkh*, V; 809 (Beirut edition), see also M.R. Salīm, *'Aṣr Salaṭīn al-Mamalik....* I; 14-21.

48. See Ibn Taghri Bardī, VI; 331

49. This implies that he considered them public property, and not the property of the Sultan.

50. *Ṭabaqāt*; V; 84-5

51. Ibn Iyās, *Badā'i al-Zuhūr*, Fol. 147, Ms. Br. Mus. al-Suyūṭī, *Ḥusn.*, II; 110

52. See Chapter, I

53. Al-Subkī, V; 101

54. Ibid, V, 101

55. See Chapter, V, Footnote, 46.

56. *Muḥammad wa 'l-Mar'a*, p. 56

57. op. cit., page 206.

58. op. cit., III; 182.

59. The play was performed by the Egyptian national theatre in January 1962 in Cairo.

60. *Al-Majalla* (Cairo), No. 62, Vol. 6 March 1962, p. 60.

61. *Al-Majalla*, Nos. 62, 63 Vol. 6 March, April 1962, articles مسرحيةالسلطان الحائر and
السلطان الطائر بين الفن والتاريخ

62. The critic was more concerned with internal and literary criticism of the play, and not put forward any historical evidence, except for the quotation from al-Subkī.

63. *Ṭabaqāt*, Fol. 72a

64. See Chapter, I.

65. In legal matters the evidence of a slave cannot be accepted, as is well known.

66. Ms. Bodleian op. cit., Biographical note on 'Izz al-Dīn. Because of a slight mistake in the title of the work and its author's *Shuhra* it has been wrongly ascribed to another person. Although there is no mention of the copyist the customary humble phrase with the author's first name suggests that it is, perhaps, an autograph copy.

67. See al-Maqrīzī, I; 226, 281, 321.

68. Ibn 'Arnus, *Tārīkh al-Qaḍā*......, p. 193

69. We must remember that a fairly detailed biography (32 pp.) of 'Izz al-Dīn by al-Hakkārī, which is mentioned by Ibn Rāfi' p. 106, and also by al-Subkī, V; 83 (he mentions the author by his *Shuhra*) is inaccessible to us. It has, probably, long been lost.

70. Correctly named by al-Ṣafadī (Vol. 19, Fol. 5a), al-Kutubī (I: 595) al-Maqrīzī, I; 312.

Al-Subkī wrongly names him Fakhr al-Dīn 'Uthmān (The correct from is Yūsuf) b...., because this brother was confined to his house by royal command in the same year, and was only released and appointed wazīr in 643 A.H. after the death of the other. See al-Maqrīzī, I; 309, 322.

71. See the article Aulād Shaykh al-Shuyūkh in El and also; al-Maqrīzī op. cit., I. 261.

72. *Al-Sulūk*, I; 318

73. Ibid. 1; 312, Ibn Wāṣil, *Mufarrij al-Kurūb*, fol. 69. Ms. Paris 1703
74. Vol. 19, Fol. 5a
75. Al-Subkī, V; 101
76. A mistake copied from al-Subkī.
77. Al-Maghribī, *Muḥammad wa 'l-Mar'a*, p. 56
78. Ibn Taghrī Bardī, VII; 72.
79. Ibn Wāṣil, *Mufarrij al-Kurūb*, fol. 145. (He was present in this assembly).
80. Ibn Taghrī Bardī, VII; 72, Ibn Iyās, I; 95.
81. Ibn Wāṣil, fol. 145. Ibn Taghrī Bardī VII; 72, Ibn Iyās, I; 95, also al-Subkī, V; 83 the latter's account is much briefer and slightly different.
82. Al-Subkī, V; 83.
83. He was al-'Ādil's grandson, was a lover of literature and had fine poetic taste. For his detailed biography see al-Yūnīnī, I; 126-177.
84. Al-Yūnīnī, I; 157 gives the date 658, A.H. which is obviously incorrect, as 'Izz al-Dīn was the Qāḍī of Egypt only in the year 640 A.H.
85. Al-Yūnīnī, I; 158, for the full text of the letter see pp. 157-159.
86. Abu 'l-Fidā, *Tā'rīkh*, III;204.
87. A military chief to whom Baybars, Rukn al-Dīn, first belonged.
88. Al-Ṣafadī, Vol. 19, Fol. 5a, Ibn Taghrī Bardī, *al-Manhal*, Vol. II, Fol. 62b Ms. Nūr 'Uthmāniya 3428.
89. Al-Subkī, V; 84, al-Isnawī, Fol. 129.
90. Al-Yūnīnī, II; 658, al-Subkī, V; 83, Ibn Kathīr, XIII; 231, etc.
91. 'Abd al-Laṭīf Ḥamza, op. cit. p. 69.

CHAPTER—VI

# CHARECTER AND PERSONALITY

After describing and discussing the different phases and activities of 'Izz al-Dīn's life, I shall now present a picture of him as an individual, pointing out his characteristic personal qualities.

## TRAITS AND DEMEANOUR

'Izz al-Dīn had pleasing features and an impressive appearance. He was also gifted with an imposing presence which inspired veneration and even awe, as shown by the following story which is related by al-Subkī.

While he was in confinement at Damascus, in a summer-house outside the city, a band of his enemies surrounded the house. His family was frightened, but 'Izz al-Dīn came out and opened the gate, saying to them: 'Welcome, guests'. They were over-awed by him and entered the house. He courteously seated them and offered them food. Their enmity instantly evaporated, and, impressed by his personality and generosity, they asked for his blessing.[1]

Another, even more striking example of his ability to inspire awe is the case, already referred to, of the enraged Mamlūk prince who had come to kill him.

He was humble in his behaviour, in spite of the honour and respect he enjoyed both from the public and from the Sulṭāns of his time. The words with which he admonished his son: 'Your father is not worthy to be killed in God's path', are an expression of his humility.

He lived simply, was unaffected in manners and appearance[2], and cared little for luxurious food and clothing.[3]

He disregarded the fashion of the time, which is still maintained by religious scholars in some countries, in that ‘he did not care very much for wearing the turban, the distinctive head-dress (of the religious leaders). He often wore an ordinary small woollen cap, and sometimes even attended royal occasions dressed like this. In fact, he put on whatever happened to be at hand, and cared nothing for ostentation.[4]

His humility and simplicity of dress did not, however, make him meek and humble in the presence of despotic monarchs, as we have frequently observed in preceeding pages, and shall see again in this chapter. He was humble and simple in manners and appearance, but was never submissive and undignified.

## MORAL COURAGE AND TENACITY

These qualities stand out in ‘Izz al-Dīn, and indeed his popular reputation rests principally upon his great courage in declaring and defending the right. Throughout his life he abundantly displayed these qualities, which inspired the bold stands he took against high authorities, and which are unfailingly insisted upon and praised by both early and late writers.

Al-Qarāfī al-Mālikī (d. 684 A.H.) says: ‘He paid no attention to kings, much less to those inferior to them, and he cared nothing for censure so long as he maintained the right.[5]

Al-Yāfi‘ī (d. 768 A.H.) eloquently praises these qualities in him and says: ‘He was a rock of faith; he would face the authorities, whoever they might be, and rebuff them even when threatened with terrifying dangers’.[6]

Tāshkuprī Zādeh later described him thus: ‘He spoke the truth and proclaimed it relentlessly. He would call the kings of Egypt by their first names in their royal courts, while the other religious doctors used to kiss their hands, and even kiss the ground before them’.[7]

We have seen several examples of his audacity in preceding pages. Here is another case which testifies to his outspoken boldness, and caused various authors to make the remarks which we have just quoted. Its authenticity is guaranteed by the method of its transmission (al-Subkī — his father, Taqī al-Dīn al-Subkī al-Bājī, 'Izz al-Dīn's pupil).

'Izz al-Dīn once attended a royal ceremonial occasion on the day of the 'Īd. He had come to pay a formal visit to the Sulṭān in the castle. The royal guards and the army stood in the foreground, and the Sulṭān was seated, surrounded by the state officials in their proper places, arranged in the customary splendour of the Egyptian Sulṭāns. The princes and dignitaries began to pay homage to the Sulṭān (al-Ṣāliḥ Najm al-Dīn) by kissing the ground before him. 'Izz al-Dīn watched, then, turning to the Sulṭān, he said loudly: 'O Ayyūb, what will be your defence before God, when He asks you: 'Did I not give you the kingdom of Egypt? and yet you allow immoral taverns to remain?" 'Is it so?' the Sulṭān meekly asked. 'Yes', said 'Izz al-Dīn, 'therre is such and such a tavern where wines are sold, and other immoral things are done, while you enjoy the pleasures of kingship'.

The army stood in silence, while 'Izz al-Dīn spoke loudly to the Sulṭān.

In reply to this criticism the Sulṭān said: 'O Sir, it is not I who have permitted the place to open; it had been there since my father's days'. 'You are, then', said 'Izz al-Dīn, one of those who say: "We found our fathers following a tradition".[8]

The narrator, al-Bājī, then asked his master why he had thus outspokenly reproved the Sulṭān on such a majestic occasion. 'Izz al-Dīn replied: 'O my son, I saw him in his magnificence, and I wished to humiliate him, lest his self-glorification should overcome him and destroy him'. 'Did you not fear him?', asked al-Bājī. 'O my son', replied 'Izz al-Dīn. 'the truth is that I visualised the glory of God Almighty, and the Sulṭān then appeared like a cat to me'.[9]

Ibn Ḥajar adds to his account the brief comment: 'The Sulṭān then had no alternative but to order its (the brothel's) removal'.

From this story we clearly see the motive which inspired 'Izz al-Dīn's disdainful treatment of monarchs. He wished to guard them from the evils of despotic arrogance. We see also the source from which he derived his exeptional courage, that is, his direct and live relationship with God, the All-Powerful.

His severe criticism of the Sulṭān becomes more amazing and impressive when we consider the latter's cruel and despotic nature. His court historian, Ibn Wāṣil, describes him as 'an awe-inspiring king, much given to self-glorification'. The Baḥrī Mamlūks, he says, 'who formed his principal power, and from whom were selected his retinue, his army commanders and his personal staff, went in awe of him, despite their power and influence. When they saw him come forth, they would tremble with fear.'[10]

Another reliable contemporary court historian, Sibṭ Ibn al-Jauzī says: 'He was overbearing and tyrannical, and he annihilated the Ashrafites[11] among others. One of his lords once said: "God knows that, when we sit in his court, we say to ourselves: 'From here we shall be taken to prison". When he imprisoned someone he would forget him, and no one would dare to speak to him about the wretched prisoner'.[12]

It was to this Sulṭān that 'Izz al-Dīn spoke so forthrightly and scornfully, at the imperial gathering, not in order to satisfy his own vanity, but in order to guide the Sulṭān and to remind him of his imperial duties. This was not the only occasion on which 'Izz al-Dīn treated this proud king so severely, for we need hardly remind the reader of two other occasions which we have already mentioned. However, this case is the most striking and it has been chosen by a celebrated modern scholar[13] to exemplify the moral courage and influential position of the sincere religious authorities of this period. We should also remember that it was this same Sulṭān who had warmly welcomed 'Izz al-Dīn to his country, and had honoured him with the highest civil post, that of chief *qāḍī*.

It is, then, with justification that al-Subkī says of 'Izz al-Dīn: 'Neither he himself, nor anybody who saw him, had seen his equal in standing for the right, or his equal in courage and sharpness of tongue.[14]

Ibn Musdī al-Andalusī, one of 'Izz al-Dīn's older pupils was impressed by the respect and influence enjoyed by his master both at the court and elsewhere, but disapproved of his criticism of the ruling powers. He says: 'He achieved whatever he desired in the way of rank and office, and did so in the most honourable way. Nevertheless, he remained sharp-tongued, inflexible and uncompromising. Although the sword is sharp, it may miss the mark, and many a horse stumbles before reaching the post.

In the same way he (Izz al-Dīn) quickly turned his back on rank and office, and thus became his own worst enemy.[15]

This criticism is obviously not objectives and is merely a personal view of 'Izz al-Dīn's material achievments. But this worldly critic forgets that 'Izz al-Dīn never cared for these coveted positions, and, in fact, ran away from them, as is shown by several such incidents in his life. It is his moral courage and his severity in dealing with unjust and oppressive authority which are the most notable features of his character and which distinguish him from the other submissive, feeble and conciliatory 'Ulamā' of his age.

Ibn Musdī had, in fact, no reason to pity him for the loss of his influential positions. In his earnest desire to uphold what was right, he consciously risked losing these positions, and, on occasion, deliberately withdrew from them.

A statesman once came to him, trying to induce him to meet the King of the time, and to become a frequent vistior at the court; such a relationship would have stabilized 'Izz al-Dīn's position and quieted his enemies. 'Izz al-Dīn listened to his persuasive advice, and replied: 'I have acquired learning in order to be an intermediary between God and his creatures; should I attend the courts of such as these?'[16]

This quotation shows how unjust and irrelevant Ibn Musdī's criticism was. In support of the truth 'Izz al-Dīn cared nothing for life, let alone rank and position. Ibn Musdi, apparently, forgot the following explicit statement of 'Izz al-Dīn from his well-known tract, *al-'Aqīda:*

'To risk one's life for the glorification of religion is recommended. It is for this reason that the Muslim soldier is prmitted to rush upon the ranks of the infidel enemy. In the same way, to risk one's soul for the establishment of good and the elimination of evil, and for the defence of the foundations of religion by argument and proof is also recommended. If someone is too timid to endanger his life, he is not obliged to do so, but it is still recommended. He who says that it is not permitted to risk one's life has missed the truth, and has strayed far from what is correct.'[17]

Indeed 'Izz al-Dīn himself, as we have seen, risked his life, in order to stand by what he believed to be right.

His intrepidity was a natural gift, which he preserved and used throughout his life, as we have seen in the preceeding chapter. The closest parallel, in recent times, to 'Izz al-Dīn we find in Jamāl al-Dīn al-Afghānī, (in the nineteenth century) who like 'Izz al-Dīn stirred whole nations with his exemplary moral courage, and slashed with his bitter tongue the absolute and despotic monarchs of various Muslim countries.

## TRUTHFULNESS AND SINCERITY

The keys to 'Izz al-Dīn's moral courage were his love of truth and his sincerity. These were the sole motives for everything he did. Truth is to be found in his relationship with the Omnipotent, and sincerity in his obedience to Him. This attachment was by no means morely conventional, formal or dogmatic. His relationship with Him was truly live and fresh, his sincerity was complete and disinterested, and he had absolute confidence in Him, The Beneficent, The Almighty.

The events I have mentioned serve as sufficient evidence for this hypothesis, and I need not repeat them here. One finds the flavour of 'Izz al-Dīn's truthfulness, his sincere devotion to God and his utter confidence in Him everywhere in his writings. In his above-mentioned tract on theology he says:

'In short, he who chooses God in his own life is chosen by God in turn. If a man seeks God's pleasure, by doing that which might displease men, God is pleased with him and makes him pleasing to men; but if he seeks the favour of men by doing that which might displease God, He is angry with him and makes him displeasing to men. God's favour is sufficient to win the favour of anyone else.

Let life be bitter, if thou art sweet to me. Let creation be angry with me, if thou art pleased with me.'[18]

His live, devoted and loving attachment to God, and his unreserved reliance upon Him gave him the strength before which Kings and princes often humbled themselves.

In like manner, he was benevolently sincere to people. He always endeavoured to direct them rightly, sovereign and subject alike. He never descended to any form of flattery or hypocrisy.

When al-Malik al-Ashraf, the Sulṭān of Damascus, was on his death-bed, 'Izz al-Dīn visited him, and al-Ashraf asked his advice, which 'Izz al-Dīn frankly gave. Al-Ashraf was, at the time, in a tent, outside the city. To demonstrate his hatred and contempt for his brother, the Sulṭān of Egypt, with whom he was then at enmity, his tent was erected facing towards Egypt, in a manner[19] which displayed that hatred. 'Izz al-Dīn frankly advised him not to sever the bonds of kinship, particularly at a time when the Tartars had begun to sweep across the Eastern Muslim countries, and the Sulṭān was seriously ill. Al-Ashraf listened to his advice and ordered the direction of the tent to be changed immediately; this was done in 'Izz al-Dīn's presence.[20]

In the famous case of the treaty between Ismā'īl and the Franks, when he forbade the arms dealers to sell arms to the Crusaders, he again acted from sincere religious motives, for he told them: 'It is forbidden to you, because you certainly know that they were buying them to fight your brother Muslims'.[21]

In all his dealings, both with his fellow men and with his Lord, his guiding motive was, as he himself announced in his letter to the King al-Ashraf, the Prophetic directive: 'to be sincerely devoted to God, to submit to his Prophet, to be a good adviser to rulers and a sincere admonisher of the public.'

He was, always ready to admit that his opponents were right, if the case was against him.

He once gave a legal decision in some case, in Cairo, but later realised that it was wrong. So he publicly announced in the city and throughout the country: 'My opinion was wrong, and none must act according to it'.[22]

He never liked to approach the courts of Kings. Sulṭān Al-Ashraf very much wished to receive him at his court, when the bitterness between them was at an end, but 'Izz al-Dīn never visited him. Afterwards, when the Sulṭān was ill, and sent for him, reminding him of the duty of a Muslim to call on his sick Muslim brother, 'Izz al-Dīn willingly yielded, as the right lay with the Sulṭān. He dutifully visited him and prayed for his health.

## PIETY AND ABSTINENCE

'Izz al-Dīn was pious by nature and led an ascetic life, as is frequently attested by early writers.[23]

Al-Ashraf resolved to recompense 'Izz al-Dīn for his earlier un-unjust persecution of him, and said: 'I witness to God that I will make him the richest of all scholars'. But 'Izz al-Dīn, as before, stayed away from the Sulṭān, and showed no intention of exploiting his generous sentiments for worldly gain.

When al-Ashraf finally obtained his only meeting with 'Izz al-Dīn, he asked his pardon and begged him to free him from all giult in the matter. 'As for freeing you from your guilt' said 'Izz al-Dīn 'I do that every night for all the people who might have harmed me in some way. And I go to my bed with no complaint against anyone. I desire that my reward should come from God and not from men: to be rewarded by God is much dearer to me than to be rewarded by his creatures'.[24]

At the end of the meeting, the Sulṭān presented 'Izz al-Dīn with the gift of a thousand Egyptian gold pieces, but he politely declined to accept it, saying: 'This visit was for the sake of God; I do not wish to sully it with any worldly thing'.[25]

When al-Ẓāhir Baybars built his magnificent college, named al-Ẓāhiriyya after him, he offered 'Izz al-Dīn a post in it. 'Izz al-Dīn, however, excused himself, saying: 'I already have a professorship in al-Ṣāliḥiyya college, and I would not like to rob others of their chance'. The king was eager to benefit him in some way and he asked 'Izz al-Dīn to endorse an endowment for his descendants. This 'Izz al-Dīn also refused, on the unselfish grounds that there were others in the town who deserved it more. Baybars said: 'There must be statutory post for them'. 'Izz al-Dīn thought a little, and said: 'If it is necessary, they should be given the post of prayer-leader'. Accordingly it was entered in the conditions of the college.[26]

Another example of 'Izz al-Dīn's piety is to be seen in the following case. The same King, Baybars, sent him a message when he was ill, asking him to appoint one of his sons to his posts. He replied: 'None of them is capable, and my post at al-Ṣāliḥiyya college should be assigned to Qāḍī Tāj al-Dīn'.[27]

This does not mean that all his sons were utterly incapable of assuming the post, for one of them, 'Abd al-Laṭīf, was a learned jurist.[28] Either he did not perhaps come up to his father's high academic standard, or 'Izz al-Dīn's conscience did not allow him to make a post in the noble profession of teaching hereditary.

Another case, or perhaps another version of this case, exemplifies even more sharply 'Izz al-Dīn's pity.

'Ibn Ḥinna[29], Baybar's wazir, called on 'Izz al-Dīn. Together with the King's greetings, the wazir conveyed to him the decree appointing his son to his post after his own death. 'He is not competent' said 'Izz al-Dīn. 'What will he live on?'. asked the Wazir. 'On God's providence', came the answer. 'We shall establish a grant for him' the other generously insisted. 'That is your affair' said 'Izz al-Dīn, and, finding no excuse, submitted.[30]

We can well imagine his austere and ascetic life, from the fact that when he left Egypt, after resigning from the honourable post of chief qāḍī, all his possessions were loaded on one ass, and he himself set out on foot. His avoidance of the Sulṭāns' courts, and his disregard for their favours and rewards speak for themselves as evidence for the genuineness of his piety and ascetiocism.

## CHARITY AND GENEROUSITY

Although 'Izz al-Dīn was not materially rich in any sense of the word, and had only a moderate income, he was generous and charitable. He gave to the poor and needy, and rewarded those who served him in any way.

There was once a famine in Damascus, and orchards were being sold cheaply. 'Izz al-Dīn's wife gave him some ornaments of hers and asked him to buy an orchard where they could resort in summer. He took the ornaments, sold them and gave away the money in charity. His wife asked him: 'Did you buy the orchard?' 'Yes', said 'Izz al-Dīn, 'I bought an orchard in paradise; I found people in distress so I gave away the money in charity'. His wife was sufficiently reasonable and kind to thank him for doing so.[31]

Al-Subkī says: 'He would sometimes tear a piece from his turban and give it to a beggar, if he had nothing else to give'.[32]

We should also remember his true generosity to al-Ashraf's wazir, to whom, for his courtesy 'Izz al-Dīn gave his own prayer mat - the only valuable belonging he had at the time. He gave it to a man who had brought him the news that he was to be persecuted, and asked his pardon for the meanness of the reward.

## WILL POWER AND SELF CONFIDENCE

From 'Izz al-Dīn's words and actions, we see that he was a determined man, and that he set high standards in every sphere of life, religious, legal, political and social. His scrupulousness in carrying out his religious observances has been illustrated earlier in the first chapter. His tenacity in theological matters is exemplified by his clash with the Ḥanbalite Sulṭān.

The various cases we have cited also demonstrate 'Izz al-Dīn's firmness in holding to his ideals. If he had interpreted things in a practical way and had sought acceptable excuses for compromise, as many religious authorities have done, he would have escaped many of the troubles which he had to face and might have lived in ease and comfort.

'Izz al-Dīn's piety, asceticism and humility did not make him passive, timid and retiring, as they have many pious asceties. When necessary, he could be active and assertive. Only a man like him could defy an infuriated king (al-Ashraf), and say to him 'God well known who knows His religion best, and who keeps His commandments. Besides, we claim to be of the chosen party of God.[33]

In the same way, he did not under-value his learning, and refused to cheapen himself for pious reasons, or to misuse his talents. His self-confidence is shown in his excuse to his host, the King of al-Karak: 'Your Kingdom is too small for my learning, and I wish to spread it abroad'.[34]

## FINE TASTE AND AFFABILITY

Together with all his serious virtues, he was gifted with good taste and affability. He appears to have had a tender heart and an aesthetic perceptiveness which made him enjoy fine poetry , write good prose and even, according to some, listen to music.[35] He also possessed a certain wit, humour and grace of speech; and was fond of quoting verses in his speech and writing.[36]

He was once passing by a ruined house in Cairo, while its debris was being cleared away. He quoted the verses:

أهاومها شلت يمينك خلها    لمعتبر أو واقف أو سائل
منازل قوم حدثتنا حديثهم    ولم أر اجلى من حديث المازل

(i.e. O you who are demolishing the house — may your hand be stayed — leave it. for one who may take a lesson, or a bystander, or The houses of a people tell us of them, one who questions. and I know no sweeter story than that told by houses).[37]

'Izz al-Dīn's theological tract provides a good example of his fondness for quoting verses to illustrate a point, a fondness mentioned by many early writers. In this short tract, which comprises only seven pages, and deals solely with religious matters, he quotes no less than thirteen verses, proverbial, gnomic and amatory. I give one example:

أمر على الديار ديار ليلى    اقبل ذا الجداد و ذا الجدارا
وما حب الديار شغفن قلبى    و لكن حب من سكن الديارا

(i.e. I pass through the land, the land of Laila,
And I kiss this wall and that wall.
It is not love for the land that torments my heart,
but love for her who once dwelled in the land).[38]

He was once asked for a religious opinion (*fatwā*) also how a person who was insulted and humiliated by the mob should defend himself. He wrote this verse in reply.

لا يسلم الشرف الرفيع من الأذى    حتى يراق على جوانبه الدم

(i.e. One's high honour is never safe from harm,
Unless one is ready to shed one's blood for it).[39]

He not only enjoyed fine poetry but he would also, occasionally, attempt to compose it, and would recite it to the company. If he could not continue with his composition he would ask one of the company or one of his pupils to complete the poem in the same rhyme and metre. He once composed a passionate mystical verse:

لو كان فيهم من عراه غرام ما عنفونى فى هواه ولامرا

(i(e. If any of them were infatuated with love,
they would not blame me and preprove me for loving him).[40]

He recited this verse to his class of pupils, and being unable to complete it, asked them to do so. Accordingly one student, Shams Din al-Aswānī, the qāḍī of Aswan (Egypt) extemporised a long poem, completing 'Izz al-Dīn's couplet, the first line of which runs:

لكنهم جهلو الزاذة حسنه و علمتها ولذا سهرت و ناموا

(i.e. But they did not see the charm of his beauty which I saw;
so I passed the night awake, while they slept).

'Izz al-Dīn listened to the poem and complimented the author, saying 'You are, then, a lawyer poet'.[41]

We have seen that 'Izz al-Dīn had leanings towards an ecstatic mysticism. It may be that his refined taste found its response and expression in the spiritual delicacy of mysticism.

However, al-Subkī (V; 102), drawing on the source just mentioned, the composer, informs us that he knew of no other verses except the one quoted. Al-Yāfi'ī, on the other hand, says : 'Notwithstanding his eminence and his great learning, he used to compose light verses'.[42] He then quotes seven verses, which had been transmitted in an unbroken *Isnād.* The first two of them are as follows:

أوجه وجهى نحوهم مستشفيا اليهم بهم منهم اذا الخطب اعيانى
فهم كاشفو ضرى و كربى و شدتى وهم فارجو همى و غمى واخزانى

These, and the remaining couplets, are, apparently, some kind of plain devotional verse, and have not sufficient literary quality to justify translating them here.

In the Berlin Catalogue of Arabic Mss., a fairly long poem (30 verses), in praise of al-Ka'ba, is ascribed to him.[43] The first verse of this, which is quoted, also shows no sign of literary merit.

An example of his humour is to be found in his nicknaming Tāj al-Dīn al-Firkāh, a pupil of his, al-Duwayk (i.e. little cock) because of his skill in debate.[44]

## EPILOGUE

We have examined 'Izz al-Dīn's life in detail, and have seen the characteristic features of his personality.

We have seen him as a zealous religious leader, instructing the public, as a vigilant observer of society, criticising and advising the ruling authorities, as a strict judge, administering the law, and as a learned scholar, teaching and compiling. In these various activities he often encountered antagonism, threats and persecution, but he cared nothing for these and persisted in his mission.

He loved the truth, upheld it in every situation, and often forced others to yield to it. His fearlessness in criticizing the absolute monarch of his time is, perhaps, more readily appreciable than his academic ability, for it was this fearlessness that made him the most impressive and influential person of his age, and which has given him a place in the history of reformers. Yet in the field of legal scholarship, too, he possessed remarkable talents, and produced much original thought.

His spirituality, his asceticism and his care for the public welfare were the secrets of his popularity with the common people and of his influence with the Sulṭāns of his time.

To sum up, the basic elements of his personality were: (1) His considerable scholarship and originality in the field of law, (2) his extraordinary moral courage and sincerity, and (3) his mystical spirituality.

Undoubtedly he deeply impressed his age with his distinguished qualities, especially with his exceptional moral courage, and he founded a school of learned men who followed in his footsteps. The study of the lives of many of his pupils clearly reveals the impression he made on them. The great Ibn Taymyya (661-728 A.H.), who lived just after 'Izz al-Dīn, was probably also inspired by his strong personality as a reformer. The two are very similar in holding fast to their religious opinions, caring nothing for persecution, and in participating in the political struggle against foreign enemies. I do not wish to compare them here, for there is, obviously, apart from this single resemblance, a basic difference in their approaches to legal thinking and in their attitudes towards mysticism. In both of these 'Izz al-Dīn resembles al-Ghazzālī, whom Ibn Taimiya often severely criticises.[45]

In view of 'Izz al-Dīn's two most outstanding personal qualities, I am tempted to describe him in the words of Iqbāl:

هو حلقهٔ یاران تو بریشم کی طرح نرم رزم حق و باطل هو تو فولاد ہے مؤمن

(i.e. In the company of friends the Believer is soft as silk,
in the clash between right and wrong he is steel).

# NOTES

1. Al-Subkī, V; 96.
2. Al-Yūnīnī, II; 172, Ibn al-'Imād, V; 302.
3. Ibn Ḥajar, Fol. 62a.
4. Al-Subkī, V; 83.
5. Margiral note, *Īḍāḥ al-Kalām*.... Ms. (Princeton), see also al-Isnawī, Fol. 129a.
6. *Mir'āt al-Janān.*, IV; 155
7. *Miftah al-Sa'āda.*, II; 213, for similar utterances also see al-Subkī, V; 80.
8. Qur'ān, XLIII; 21 'and followed them'. This will be the excuse of the idolators on the judgement day.
9. Al-Subkī, V; 81, 82, al-Isnawī, Fol. 129a, Ibn Ḥajar, Fol. 62.
10. 'Ibn Taghrī Bardī, VI; 331.
11. An army of Najm al-Dīn whose rebellion he feared.
12. Ibn Taghrī Bardī, VI; 333, see also his quotations from the other authors, VI; 334-5.
13. Aḥmad Amīn, *Ẓuhr al-Islām*, IV; 214. He also alludes to many other similar cases of 'Izz al-Dīn's courage.
14. Al-Subkī, V; 80
15. Ibn Rāfi', p. 106
16. 'Izz al-Dīn, *Fawā'id al-'Izz*, marginal notes. Ms. Qairo, Tafsīr 77, (unnumbered). The King alluded to seems, certainly, to be al-Ashraf of Damascus, as the mention of 'Izz al-Dīn's enemies suggests.
17. Al-Subkī, 5; 91.
18. Al-Subkī, V; 91, the verse quoted by the author is a popular one by Abu Firas al-Ḥamadanī.
19. The original text reads: 'And he placed its Dihlīz (i.e. footway or shoeplace) towards Egypt. This was, perhaps, a customary way of showing contempt for a king.
20. Al-Subkī, V; 99
21. Ibid., V; 100.
22. Al-Subkī, V; 83.
23. See al-Ṣafadī, Vol. 19 Fol. 4a Ms. Aḥmad III., Ibn al-'Imād, V; 302 etc.
24. Al-Subkī, V; 98.

25. Al-Subkī, V; 99.

26. Al-Isnawī, Fol. 129a Ms. Camb. The offer was made before the completion of the college (started in 660 A.H., it was completed in 662 A.H. (al-Maqrīzī, *al-Khiṭaṭ*, II; 378). Hence the conditions of the post. In fact, 'Izz al-Dīn's son Sharf al-Dīn was, under these conditions *Imām* in that college.

27. Al-Kutubī, I; 595, al-Yūnīnī, II; 174 etc. the person nominated was a good student of 'Izz al-Dīn, and was his deputy for some time.

28· See Chapter, I.

29. Bahā' al-Dīn, also the wazīr of Baybars' son, d. 677 A.H.

30. This interesting conversation was transmitted by an eye witness, Ibn Ḥinnās' son, Fakhr al-Dīn al-Khalīlī, and preserved with details of the date, 696 A.H., and the place, the latter's house in al-Ghaur, by al-Yūnīnī, who was personally told of the case, *Dhayl*.., I; 506. It seems likely that this was a separate case from the one just mentioned, since the offer was for one son, not both. It seems that Baybars, having provided a livlihood for one son, wished to benefit the other as well, and did so in this way.

31. Al-Subkī, V; 82-83.

32. Ibid., V; 83.

33. See Chapter, V.

34. Al-Subkī, V; 101.

35. See Chapter, IV.

36. Ibn Kathīr, XII; 235, al-Yūnīnī, II; 75, Ibn al-'Imād, V; 302.

37. Al-Yūnīnī II; 175. The verses are by 'Abd al-Wāḥid b. al-Faraj al Ma'arrī (d. 481 A.H.) He composed them in lamentation of a palace in the city of al-Ma'arra, Syria.

38. Al-Subkī, V; 96.

39. Al-Ṣāqā'ī, *Tālī Wafayāt al-A'yān*, Fol. 45b Ms. Paris, 2061. In a short biographical note of about 4 lines the only significant thing recorded by this author is this case, and he is unique in quoting it.

40. Al-Subkī, V; 102 reported in an *Isnād* of two authorities.

41. Al-Subkī V; 102. He quotes a few verses.

42. Al-Yāfi'ī, IV; 157

43. See page 59 above

44. Al-Kutubī, I; 532.

45. See, his Rasā'il, V; 10

# BIBLIOGRAPHY


*'Izz al-Dīn's works:*

1. *al-Ishāra ila 'l-Ījāz fī Ba'ḍ Anwā' al-Majāz* (*Majāz al-Qur'ān*). *Istanbul,* 1313 *A.H.*
2. *Qawā'd al-Aḥkām fī Maṣāliḥ al-Anām*, Cairo 1934 Ḥussainiya publishing house (also al-Makṭaba al-Tijariyya ed. n.d.)

**Manuscripts**

| | | |
|---|---|---|
| 3. | Br. Mus. Add. 9691 | *Majāz al-Qur'ān* |
| 4. | Br. Mus. Add. 3096 | *Qawā'id al-Sharī'a* |
| 5. | Cairo, Tafsīr 32 | *Tafsīr al-Qur'ān* |
| 6. | Chester Beatty 3184 (2) | *Ḥall Maqāṣid al-Ri'āya* |
| 7. | Damascus (Ẓāhiriyya), Fiqh Shāfi'ite 60 | *al-Fawā'id fī Mukhtaṣar al-Qawā'id* |
| 8. | ,, Ẓāhiriyya, 119 | *al-Qawā'id al-Kubrā* |
| 9. | ,, Ẓāhiriyya, 4605 | *Targhīb Ahl al-Islām fī Sukna 'l-Shām* |
| | ,, Ẓāhiriyya, 1914 | Another copy |
| 10. | ,, Ẓāhiriyya, 5258 | *Waṣiyya* |
| 11. | Escorial 1536 (1) | *Sharjarat al-Ma'ārif wa 'l-Aḥwāl wa Ṣāliḥ al-A'māl wa 'l-Aqwāl* |
| 12. | ,, ,, (2) | *al-Farq Bayn al-Īmān wa 'l-Islām* |
| 13. | ,, ,, (3) | *Bidaya al-sa'ūl fī Tafḍīl al-Rasūl* |
| 14. | ,, ,, (4) | *Maqāṣid al-Ṣalā* |
| 15. | ,, ,, (5) | *Kitāb al-Ṣawm* |
| 16. | ,, ,, (6) | *Manāsik al-Ḥajj* |
| 17. | ,, ,, (7) | *al-Fitan wa 'l-Balāya* |

## GENERAL BIBLIOGRAPHY

**Manuscripts**


| | | |
|---|---|---|
| * al-'Āmirī | : | 'Imād al-Dīn Yaḥyā: *Ghirbāl al-Zamān* Br. Ms. Add. 21,587 |
| * Anon | : | *Qiṣṣat Ibn 'Abd al-Salām,* Leyden, or 644 (27) |
| * ” | : | *A history of the Ayyubids,* Cambridge, Add. 2955 |
| * ” | : | *al-Wulāt wa 'l-Quḍāt fī 'l-Islām* |
| * ” | : | *Risāla fī 'l-Tarājim.* Ẓāhiriyya, 4612 |
| * ” | : | *Manāqib al-Shaykh 'Izz al-Dīn 'Abd al-Salām.* Princeton. MS. Gareett 1165, H. |
| Ibn 'Aṭiyya | : | *al-Jāmi' al-Muḥarra al-Wajīz* (*Tafsīr*), Br. Mus. or 4746 |
| al-Dhahabī | : | *Siyar al-Nubalā',* (Istanbul) Aḥmad III. 2910 |
| * ” | : | *al-'Ibar fī Akhbār man Ghabar* (*with the* supplement of al-Ḥusayni) Bodleian, Laud A. 109 |
| Ibn Ghanim | : | 'Izz al-Dīn 'Abd al-Salām al-Wā'iẓ al-Maqdisī: *Ḥall al-Rumūz wa Miftāḥ al-Kunūz* Bodleian, Hunt 222 |
| * Ibn Ḥabīb | : | (al-Ḥalabī), Badr al-Dīn al-Ḥasan: *Durrat al-Asluk.* Bodl. Marsh 223 |
| * Ibn Ḥajar | : | (al-'Asqalānī) *Raf' al-Iṣr 'an quḍāt Miṣr,* Istanbul, Faiḍ. 1400 |
| * al-Isnawī | : | 'Abd al-Raḥīm b al-Ḥasan: *Ṭabqāt al-Shāfi'iyya,* Cambridge, or 843 |
| * al-Manṣūrī | : | Rukn al-Dīn Baybars: *Zubdat al-Fikra,* Br. Mus. Add. 23, 325 |
| * Ibn al-Mulaqqin | : | Sharf al-Dīn Abū Ḥafṣ: *Ṭabaqāt al-Shāfi'iyya* Bodlian, Hunt, 108 |

| | | |
|---|---|---|
| * Ibn Qāḍī Shuhba | : | Taqī al-Dīn Abū Bakr b. Aḥmad: *Tabaqāt al-Shāfi'iyya,* Br. Mus. Add. 23,362 |
| * al-Ṣafadī | : | Ṣālaḥ al-Dīn Khalīl b. Aybak: *al-Wafī bi 'l-Wafayāt,* Vol. 5 Bodleian, Aroh. Sold. A. 20; Vol. 19 Istanbul, Aḥmad III. 2920 |
| * al-Ṣaqa'ī | : | Muwaqaf al-Dīn Faḍl Allāh b. Fakhr (d. 725 A.H.): *Tālī Wafayāt al-A'yān,* Paris. 2061 |
| * Sibṭ Ibn Ḥajar | : | Jamāl al-Dīn Yūsuf b. Shāhīn: *al-Nujūm al-Zāhira Br.* Mus. Add. 23,360 |
| Sharaf al-Din | : | Muḥammad b. 'Izz al-Dīn al-Sulamī: *Iḍāḥ al-Kalām fī Mas'alat al-Kalām.* Princeton. Yahuda, 1847 |
| al-Suyūṭī | : | *Tanbi'at al-Ghabī bi Tabri'at-i Ibn 'Arabi.* Ẓāhiriyya, 5258 |
| * Ibn Wāṣil | : | Jamāl al-Dīn Muḥammad (d. 695 A.H.), *Mufarrij al-Kurūb.* Paris 1703 |

**Printed Books**

| | | |
|---|---|---|
| Amīn, Aḥmad | : | *Ḍuḥa 'l-Islām* 3 vol. Cairo 1952 |
| ,, ,, | : | *Ẓuhr al-Islām* 4 vol. Cairo 1953 |
| ,, ,, | : | — 1955 |
| Ibn al-Anbarī | : | Abu 'l-Barkāt 'Abd al-Raḥmān, *al-Inṣāf fī Masā'l al-Khilāf.* ed. G. Weit. Leyden 1913 |
| Ibn 'Arabī | : | Muḥyi al-Dīn: *Diwān.* Bombay n.d. |
| Arberry A.J. | : | *The Koran Interperated* 2 vols. London 1955 |
| * Ibn 'Arnus | : | Maḥmūd b. Muḥammad: *Tārīkh al-Qaḍā fī 'l-Islām,* Cairo 1934 |
| al-'Aṣkarī | : | Abū Hilāl: *al-Furūq al-Lughawiyya.* Cairo 1353 A.H. |
| al-Aṣma'ī | : | 'Abd al-Malik b. Qarīb: *al-Mufaḍḍaliyat,* ed. Loyal, Oxford 1921; indices by Bevan Leyden. 1924 |
| Ibn Aṭā' Allāh | : | Tāj al-Dīn: *Laṭā'if al-Minan* Cairo 1313 |

A.H. (on the margin of *Laṭā'if al-Minan* by al-Sha'rānī)

Ibn Athaīr : 'Izz al-Dīn 'Alī b. Muḥammad: *al-Lubāb fī Tadhkirat al-Ansāb*, Cairo, 1357/1938

al-Bābānī : Ismā'īl Pāshā al-Baghdādī: *Dhail Kashf al-Ẓunūn*. Anqara 1945

„ : *Hadiyyat al-'Ārifīn*. 2 vols. Anqara 1951.

al-Bāqillānī : Abū Bakr Muḥammad b. al-Ṭayyib: *I'jāz al-Qur'ān*, ed. Aḥmad al-Ṣaqr. Cairo 1949

* Brockelmann, C : *Geschichte der Arabischen Litteratur*. *Leyden* 1931-1949

al-Bukhārī : *Saḥiḥ* 4 vols. Leyden 1868

Cahencl : Article "Ayyūbids" in *Encyclopeadia of Islam* (New Edition) Leyden 1958

al-Dānī, : Abū 'Amr b Uthmān: *al-Tāisīr fī l-Qirā'āt al-Sab'*, ed. Otto partzh. Istanbul 1938

Abū Dāwūd : *Sunan* (with the commentary by al-Kahṭṭabī) 8 vols. Cairo 1948-50

al-Dhahabī, : al-Ḥāfiẓ Shams al-Dīn: *Duwal al-Islam*, Hyderabad. 1337 A.H.

Diwān al-A'shā, : ed. R. Geyer. Wien - 1927 (Gibb Mem, New Series - VI)

Diwān Imr'al-Qays : ed. Abu'l-Faḍl Muḥammad Ibrahim, Cairo, 1958

Diwān Labīd, : ed. Yūsuf Ḍiyā' al-Dīn al-Maqdisī, Wien. 1880

al-Farrā' : Yaḥyā b. Ziyād (d. 207 A.H.): *Ma'ani al-Qur'ān* vol. I ed. A.H. Nijati Cairo, 1955 (In progress)

* Ibn abi 'l-Faḍā'il : Mufaḍḍal: *al-Nahj al-Sadīd, ed. E.* Blochet (In Patrolgia Orientalis XII) Paris 1919

Ibn Faris, : Abu'l -Ḥussayn Aḥmad (d. 395 A.H.) *Mu'jam Maqā'īs al-Lugha* 6 vols. ed. 'Abd al-Salām Ḥarūn. Cairo 1947-52.

* al-Fāsī, : Ḥasan b. Muḥammad al-Kohen: *Ṭabaqāt al-Shādhiliyya*, Cairo 1347 A.H.

al- Bukhārī : *Saḥiḥ* 4 vols. Leyden 1868

Cahen cl : Article "Ayyubids" in *Encyclopaedia of Islām* (New Edition) Leyden 1958

al-Dānī, : Abū 'Amr b. Uthmān: *al-Taisīr fī l-Qirā'āt al-Sab'*, ed. Otto partzh. Istạnbul 1938

Abu Dāwūd : *Sunan* (with the commentary by al-Khaṭṭabi) 8 vols. Cairo 1948-50

al-Dhahabī, : *Duwal al-Islām*. Hyderabad. 1337 A.H.

Diwān al-A'shā, : ed. R. Geyer. Wien - 1927 (Gibb Mem. New Series - VI)

Diwān Imru'al-Qais : ed. Abu'l-Faḍl Muḥammad Ibrahimi. Cairo; 1958

Diwān Labīd, : ed. Yūsūf Ḍiyā' al-Dīn al-Maqdisi, Wien. 1880

al-Farrā' : Yaḥyā b. Ziyād (d. 207 A.H.): *Ma'ani al-Qur'ān* vol. I ed. A.H. Nijati Cario, 1955 (In progress)

* Ibn Abi 'l-Faḍā'il : Mufaḍḍal: *al-Nahj al-Sadīd*, ed. E. Blochet (In Patrolgia Orientalis XII) Paris 1919

Ibn Fāris, : Abu 'l-Ḥusain Aḥmad (d. 395 A.H.) *Mu'jam Madā'is al-Lugha* 6 vols. ed. 'Abd al-Salām Harūn. Cairo 1947-52.

* al-Fāṣī, : Ḥasan b. Muḥammad al-Kohen: *Ṭabaqāt al-Shadhiliyya*. Cairo 1347 A.H.

* Abu'l-Fidā' : *al-Mukhtaṣar fī Akhbār al-Be-Shar*. 4 vols. Istanbul. 1286 A.H.

Ibn Farḥūn, : Burhān al-Dīn Ibrāhīm b. 'Alī: *al-Dibāj al-Mudhahhab*. Cairo 1329 A.H.

Flūgel. : G: *Concordinatiae Corani Arabicae Leipzig*, 1875

Ibn al-Furāt, : Nāṣir al-Dīn Muḥammad: *Tārīkh,* ed. Dr. Q: Zuraiq vols. 7, 8 Beirut 1932

Ḥajjī Khalīfa : *Kashf al-Ẓunun* 2 vols. Anqara 1941 (also Flugel's edition Leipzing 1835-58).

Ibn Ḥajar : (al-'Asqaiani): *al-Durar al-Kāmina* 4 vols. Hyderabad. 1348-50 A.H.

" : *Lisān al-Mīzan.* 6 vols. Hyderabad. 1329-31 A.H.

* Ḥamza, : Dr. 'Abd al-Laṭīf: *al-Ḥaraka al-Fikriyya fī al-Daulat al-Ayyūbiya wa 'l-Mamlūkiyya.* Cairo.

Ibn Ḥanbal : *Musnad,* 6 vols. Cairo 1313 A.H. ed. Aḥmad Shākir 15 vols. Cairo 1954-56.

Ibn Ḥazm : *al-Muḥalla* 10 vols. Cairo 1352 A.H.

Ibn Hishām : *al-Sīra al-Nabawiyya,* 2 vols. ed. M. al-Saqqa etc. 1955.

Hitti, P.K. : *History of the Arabs,* London 1956

Ibn Ḥujja : (al-Hamawī): *Thmarāt al-Aurāq,* Cairo. 1300 A.H.

* Ibn 'l-'Imād, : 'Abd al-Ḥayy al-Ḥanbalī: *Shadharāt al-Dhahab,* 8 vols. Cairo 1351 A.H.

* Ibn Iyās : Aḥamd al-Miṣrī: *Tārīkh Miṣr* (Badā'i' al-Zuhur), Cairo 1311 A.H.

Ibn al-Jazarī, Shams al-Dīn Muḥammad: *Ghūyat al-Nihāya fī Ṭabaqāt al-Qurra',* 2 vols. (3rd volum, indices) ed. Bergstrassr. Cairo 1933-35

* Ibn Kathīr : *al-Bidaya wa 'l-Nihāya,* 13 vols. Cairo 1932-39

* Kaḥḥāla, 'Umar Riḍa: *mu'jam al-Mu'allifīn* 12 vols. Damascus. 1959-61 (In progress)

Ibn Khaldūn : *Muqaddima,* Cairo 1322 A.H.

„ : *Tārīkh,* 10 vols. Beirut 1956-9

Ibn Khālawaih : *al-Qirā'at al-Shādhdha* ed. Bergstrasser. Cairo 1934

Ibn Khallikān : *Wafayāt al-A'yān* 2 vols. Cairo 1310 A.H. (also de Slane's translated edition 4 vols).

al-Khuḍrī : Muḥammad: *Tārīkh al-Tashrī' al-Islāmi.* Cairo 1st Edition n.d.

* al-Maghribī, : 'Abd al-Qādir: *Muḥammad wa 'l-Mar'a.* Damascus n.d.

Ibn Māja : *Sunan.* ed. F. 'Abd al-Bāqī, 2 vols. Cairo. 1955-56

Mālik : *Mw'aṭṭa',* (with al-Suyūṭī's commentary *Tanwir al-Ḥawālik*) 2 vols. Cairo 1348 A.H.

Ibn Manẓūr : *Lisān al-'Arab.* 15 vols. Beirut 1955-56 also Bulaq edition.

al-Maqqarī : *Nafḥ al-Ṭīb* 2 vols. ed. Dozy. W. Right etc. Leyden 1855-61

* al-Mqrīzī : *al-Sulūk fī Ma'rifat Duwal al-Mulūk,* ed. Dr. M. Ziyada 2 vols. Cairo 1934

* „ : *al-Khiṭaṭ,* 2 vols. Cairo 1270 A.H.

* al-Marāghī, : A.A. al-Fatḥ: *al-Mubīn fī Ṭabaqāt al-Uṣūliyyin.* Cairo n.d. (recent publication)

al-Marzubānī : *Mu'jam al-Shu'arā',* ed. A.S. Farraj. Cairo 1960

Mubārak, : Zakī: *al-Taṣawuf al-Islāmī* 2 vols. Cairo 1954

* al-Muṣannif, : Abū Bakr Hidāyat Allāh: *Ṭabaqāt al-Shāfi'iyya,* Baghdād, 1356. A.H.

Muslim : *Ṣaḥiḥ,* ed. F. Abd al-Baqī 5 vols. (5th indices) Cairo 1955-56

* al-Nabhānī, : Yūsuf b. Ismā'īl: *Jāmi' Karāmāt al-Auliyā'.* Cairo 1329 A.H.

al-Nasafī, : Abu 'l-Barakāt 'Abd Allāh, *Tafsīr* (*Madārik al-Tanzīl*), 3 vols. Cairo 1326 A.H.

al-Nadwī, : Riḍwān 'Alī: al-'Izz b.'Abd al-Salām, Damascus 1960 ed. A. Ja'far

* al-Nu'imī, : 'Abd al-Qādir: *al-Dāris*, al-Ḥusainī. Damascus 1948

Nicholson, : R.A.: *Studies in Islamic Mysticism*, Cambridge 1921

,, : *Mystics of Islam*, London 1914

al-Qārī : (al-Baghdādī) Ibrāhīm b. 'Abd Allāh: *Manāqib Ibn 'Arabī. ed. Dr.* S.D. al-Munajjid. Beirut. 1961

al-Qifṭī : *Inbāh al-Ruwā fī Akhbār al-Nuha* 3 vols. ed. Abu 'L-Fadl Ibrāhim, Cairo, 1950-55

al-Qurṭubī : *Tafsīr* (al-Jāmi' li Aḥkām al-Qur'ān) 20 vols. Cairo 1933-50.

Ibn Qatayba : *Ta'wīl Mushkil al-Qur'ān* ed. Aḥmad al-Ṣaqr. Cairo 1954

al-Raḍī : (—al-Sharīf): *Talkhis al-Bayān fī Majāzāt al-Qur'ān, ed. 'Abd 'l-Ghanī Ḥasan,* Cairo, 1955

* al-Rafi'ī, : *Muṣtafā Ṣādiq; Wahyi al-Qalam*, Cairo (al-Maktaba al-Tijariyya) N.D.

* Ibn Rāfi' : (al-Salamī), Abu 'l-Ma'ālī Muḥammad: *Tārīkh 'Ulamā' Baghdād*. Baghdād 1357 A.H.

al-Rāghib : (al-Iṣfahānī): *al-Mufradāt*, Cairo, 1324 A.H.

Ibn Rajab : *Ṭabaqāt al-Ḥanābila*, 2 vols, Cairo, 1952-53

al-Rāzī : *Tafsīr*. 8 vols. Cairo, 1307 A.H.

al-Ṣafadī, : Ṣālaḥ al-Dīn Khalīl: *al-Wāfī bi 'l-Wafayāt*. Vol. I. ed. Ritter, Istanbul, 1949. Vols. 2,3,4, ed. Dedering, Istanbul, 1953. Vols. 3,4, Damascus, 1958-9

al-Sakhāwī : *al-Ḍau' al-Lāmi'*, 12 vols. Cairo, 1353-55 A.H.

Ṣāliḥ, : Dr. Subḥī: *Mabāḥith fī 'Ulūm al-Qur'ān*, Damascus 1958

Ibn Salāma, : Abu 'l-Qāsim Hibat Allāh (d. 410 A.H.) *al-Nāsikh wa 'l-Mansūkh* (on the margin of al Wāḥidī's Aṣbāb al-Nuzūl, Cairo, 1315 A.H.)

* Sālim, : Maḥmūd Ruziq: *'Aṣr Salaṭīn al-Mamālīk wa Intājuhu al-'Ilmi wa 'l-Adabī*, 3 *vols.* Cairo 1947

* Sarkīs, : Ilyan. *Mu'jam al-Matbū'āt al-'Arabiyya*, Cairo 1928

* Abū Shāmma, : Shihāb al-Dīn al-Maqdisī: *al-Rauḍatayn.* Cario 1287 .A.H.

* „ : *Tarājim Rijāl al-Qarnayn al-Sādis wa 'l-Sābi'* (*Dail al-Rauaḍatyan*), Cairo 1947

al-Sha'rānī, : 'Abd al-Wahhāb: *al-Ṭabaqāt al-Kubrā* (Lawaqih al-Anwār), Cairo, 1925

„ : *al-Yawāqīt wa 'l-jawāhir*, Cairo

al-Shalabī, : Dr. 'Abd al-Fattāḥ: *Abū 'Alī al-Fārisī* (Doctoral thesis) Cairo 1958.

* Sibṭ Ibn al-Jauzī : *Mir'āt al-Zamān*, Vol. 8 Hyderabad. 1951

Sībawaih : *al-Kitāb*, ed. G. Jahn. 2 vols. Berlin 1895

al-Sijistānī, : Abū Bakr 'Abd Allāh b. Abī Dāwūd: *Kitāb al-Maṣāḥif.* ed. A. Jeffery, Cairo, 1936

Smith, : Dr. Margaret: *An early mystic of Baghdad*, London 1935.

* al-Subkī, : Tāj al-Dīn 'Abd 'l-Wahhāb: *Ṭabaqāt al-Shāfi'iyya*, 6 vols. Cairo 1324 A.H.

al-Suyūṭī : *al-Itqān fī 'Ulūm al-Qur'ān*, Cairo 1360 A.H.

* al-Suyūṭī : *Ḥusn al-Muḥāḍara*. 2 vols. Cairo 1299 A.H. (also the edition 1321 A.H.)

| | | |
|---|---|---|
| ,, | : | *al-Ashbāh wa 'l-Naẓā'ir al-Naḥwiyya,* Hyderabad 1359/1940 |
| ,, | : | *al-Ashbāh wa 'l-Naẓā'ir al-Fiqḥiyya,* Cairo |
| ,, | : | *al-Durr al-Manthūr-(Tafsīr)* 6 vols. in 3 Tehran, 1958 |
| ,, | : | *Ṭabaqāt al-Mufassirīn,* ed. Moursinge Lugd. Bat. 1839 |
| al-Ṭabarī | : | *Tafsīr (Jāmi' al-Bayān)* 15 vols. ed. Maḥmūd Shākir. Cairo 1956-61 (in progress) also old edition, 30 vols. |
| * Ibn Taghrī Bardī | : | Abu'l-Maḥāsin: *al-Nujūm al-Zāhira* 9 vols. Cairo 1929-1942 |
| * ,, | : | *al-Manhal al-Ṣāfī,* extracted and translated by G. Wiet. Cairo 1932 (memoires A.L. Institute D'Egypt XIX) |
| Ibn Taimiya | : | *al-Rasā'il,* ed. Rashīd Riḍā, 5 vols. Cairo 1341-49 A.H. |
| ,, | : | *al-Radd al-'l-Manṭiqiyyin,* Bombay, 1949. |
| * Ṭanṭawī, | : | 'Alī: *Min Rijāl al-Tārīkh,* Damascus 1958 |
| * Tashku prīzādeh, | : | Aḥmad b. Muṣṭafā: *Miftāḥ al-Sa'āda* 2 vols. Hyderabad 1329 A.H. |
| Tritton, | : | A.S.: *Materials on Muslim education in the Middle Ages,* London 1951 |
| al-Tirmidhī | : | *Al-Jāmi' al-Ṣaḥīḥ,* ed. Aḥmad Shākir F.A. Baqī. 4 vols. Cairo 1937-1958 |
| Ibn Ṭūlūn, | : | Qāḍī Shams al-Dīn: *Quḍāt Dimashq.* Damascus 1956 |
| Abū 'Ubayda, | : | Ma'mar b. al-Muthannā (d. 210 A.H.) *Majāz al-Qur'ān,* ed. Fu'ād Segsin Cairo 1954 |
| al-Wāḥidī, | : | Abu 'l-Ḥasan 'Alī b. Aḥmad al-Nisābūri: *Asbāb al-Nuzūl.* Cairo. 1315 A.H. |
| Ibn Wāṣil, | : | Jamāl al-Dīn Muḥammad: *Mufarrij al-Kurūb,* ed. Dr. J. al-Shayyal. 3 vols. Cairo 1953 - (in progress) |

Wensinck : *Concordance de la Tradition Musulman* 3 vols. Leyden, 19 (in progress)

* al-Yāfi'ī, : 'Abd Allāh b. As'ad: *Mir'āt al-Janān* 4 vols. Hyderabad 1337 A.H.

* ,, : *Nashr al-Mahasin al-Ghaliya fī fada'il al-Sufiyya* 2 vols. Cairo 1329 A.H.

Yāqūt : *Mu'jam al-Buldān,* 6 vols. Leipzig 1866-78 *Irshād al-Arib* 7 Vols. ed. Margoliouth

,, : Leyden-London 1907 - 1926

* al-Yūnīnī, : Quṭb al-Dīn Mūsa (d. 726 A.H.): *Dhail Mir'āt al-Zamān,* 2 vols. Hyderabad. 1954-55

al-Zabīdī, : al-Sayyid Murtaḍā: *Tāj al-'Arūs* 10 vols.

Zaid, : Muṣṭafā: *Lectures on Uṣūl al-Fiqh.* Damascus University 1958-59 (unpublished)

Ibn Zainī Daḥlān : *al-Futūḥāt al-Islāmiyya,* Mecca, 1302 A.H.

al-Zamakhsharī : *al-Kashshāf* 3 vols. Cairo 1318-19 A.H. (also edition 1307 A.H), 2 vols)

* al-Zarkalī, : Khair al-Dīn: *Qamūs al-A'Lām* 10 vols. Damascus 1956-59

Al-Zamakhsharī : *Lisān al-Balāgha* 2 vols. Cairo 1922

al-Zarqā', : Muṣṭafā: *al-Madkhal al-Fiqhī al-'Āmm,* 2 vols. 1958

Abū Zuhra, : Muḥammad: *Ibn Taymiya,* Cairo 1955

,, : al-Shāfi'ī, Cairo 1945


*The books which are marked **
*contain notices of the life of the author.*

## CATALOGUES OF MSS


| | | |
|---|---|---|
| Arab League Inst. | : | *Catalogue of Photo prints* by F. Sayyid, Cairo 1952 |
| Baghdad, | : | (Auqāf Library): *al-Kashshāf:* by M.A. Talas. Baghdad 1953 |
| Banikpur (India) | : | 35 vols. by M.A. Nadwī and others Calcutta 1908-42 |
| Berlin | : | 10 vols. by W. Ahlwardt. Berlin 1887-99 |
| Bodleian | : | 2 vols. by Uri and Nicholl 1737, 1821 |
| British Museum | : | 2 vols. London 1846-71 |
| ,, | : | Supplement by Rieu. London 1894 |
| Brill | : | Vols. by M. Th Houtsma Leyden, 1886-89 |
| Cambridge | : | by E.G. Browne Cambridge 1900 |
| ,, | : | Supplement by E.G. Browne Cambridge 1922 |
| ,, | : | 2nd supplement by Prof A.J. Arberry Cambridge 1952 |
| Cairo | : | First Catalogue by al-Bablāwī etc. Cairo 1301-1308 A.H. |
| Chester Beatty | : | 4 vols. by A.J. Arberry. Dublin 1955-58 |
| Escorial (Madrid) | : | 3 vols. in 4 by Derenbourg and others. Paris 1884-1941 |
| Gohta | : | 4 vols. by W. Pertsch. Vienna, 1878-83 |
| Istanbul | : | "*Dafatir*" of the Mosque Libraries 4 Vols. Istanbul 1893 Topkapi Sarayi by F.E. Kartay 2 Vols. Istanbul 1961 |
| Leyden | : | 6 Vols. by Dozy and others. Leyden 1851-1889 |
| Mauşil | : | By Dr. D. Chalapī, Mauşil |
| Paris | : | By de Slane, Paris 1883-95 |
| ,, | : | By E. Blochet. Paris 1909 |
| Taimuriyya Collection | : | (Cairo) 4 Vols. by M.J. al-Asm'i. Cairo 1948-50 |

| | | |
|---|---|---|
| Rabāṭ | : | by Levi-Provencal. Paris 1921- by Ragragi and Allouche. Paris 1954 |
| Vienna | : | 3 Vols by G. Flügel - Wien 1865-67 |
| Ẓāhiriyya | : | (Damascus) by H. Zayyat Cairo 1902 |
| ,, | : | Present handwritten list. |

# INDEX

*Prepared by*
Muhammad Tufail
Research Fellow IRI